IF IT'S NOT FUNNY IT'S ART

DRAWINGS BY DEMETRI MARTIN

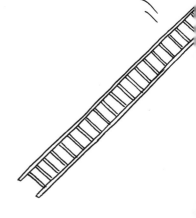

GRAND CENTRAL
PUBLISHING

NEW YORK   BOSTON

Grand Central Publishing
Hachette Book Group
1290 Avenue of the Americas, New York, NY 10104
grandcentralpublishing.com
twitter.com/grandcentralpub

First edition: September 2017

Grand Central Publishing is a division of Hachette Book Group, Inc. The Grand Central Publishing name and logo is a trademark of Hachette Book Group, Inc.

The publisher is not responsible for websites (or their content) that are not owned by the publisher.

The Hachette Speakers Bureau provides a wide range of authors for speaking events. To find out more, go to www.hachettespeakersbureau.com or call (866) 376-6591.

Library of Congress Control Number: 2017948603

ISBNs: 978-1-5387-2904-5 (trade paperback), 978-1-5387-2905-2 (ebook)

Printed in the United States of America

LSC-C

10 9 8 7 6 5 4 3 2 1

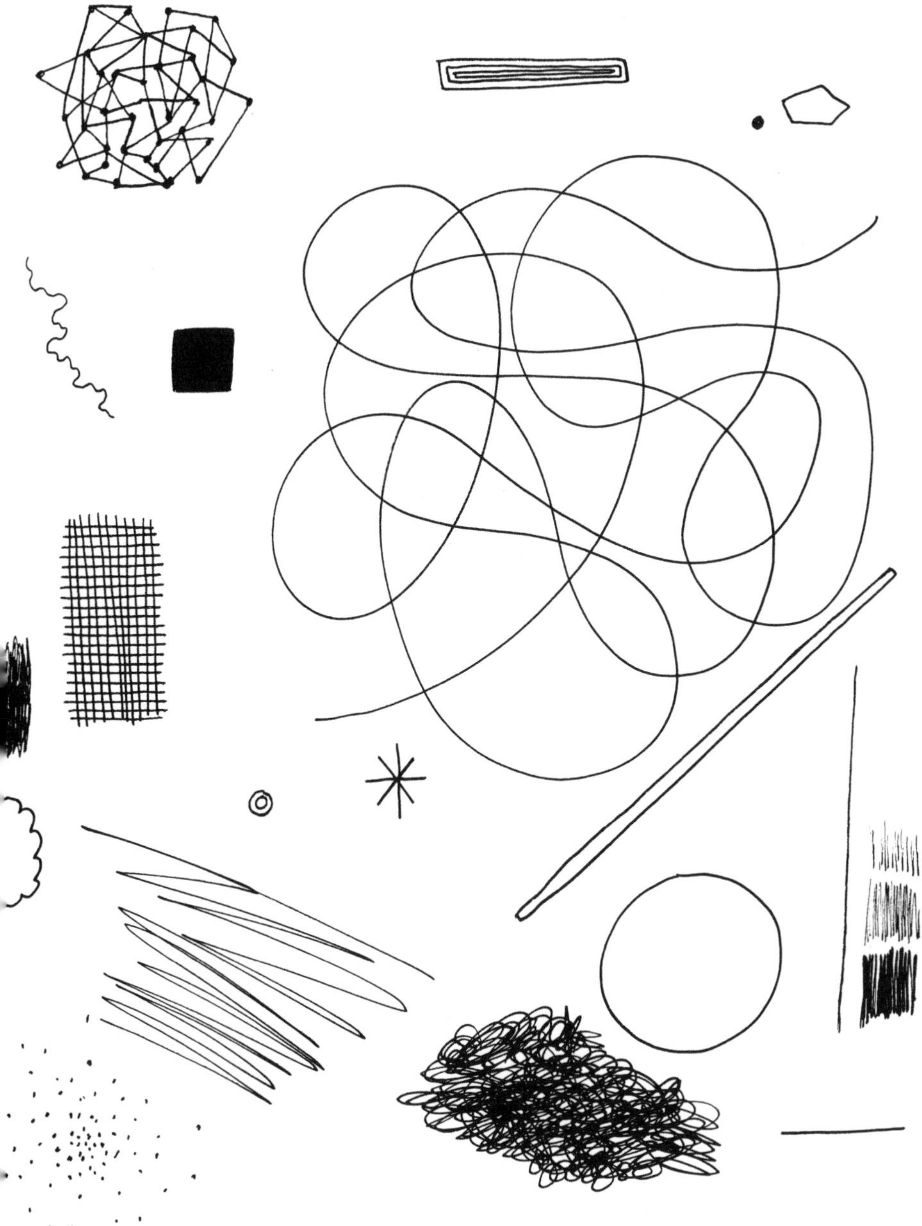

(Just Testing Pen)

Stretching for Upcoming Scenes in Book

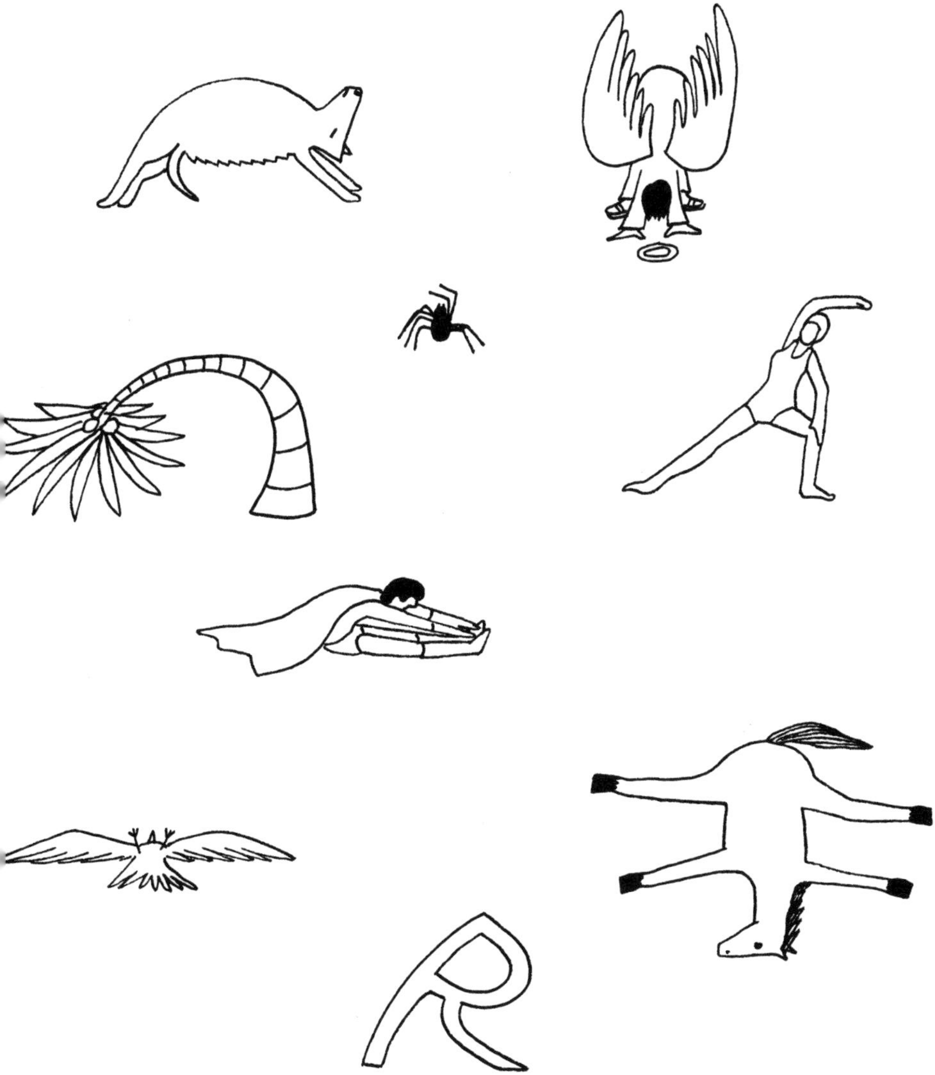

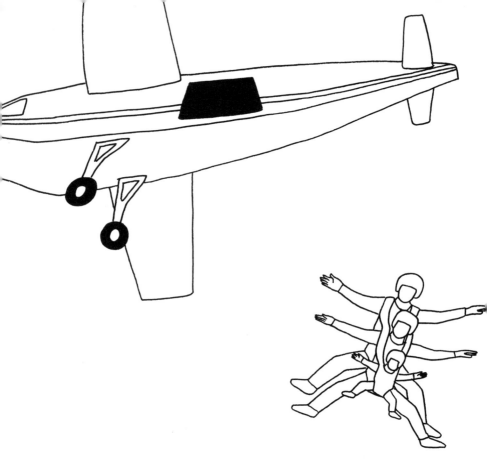

Man Poses for Selfie
During Moral Dilemma

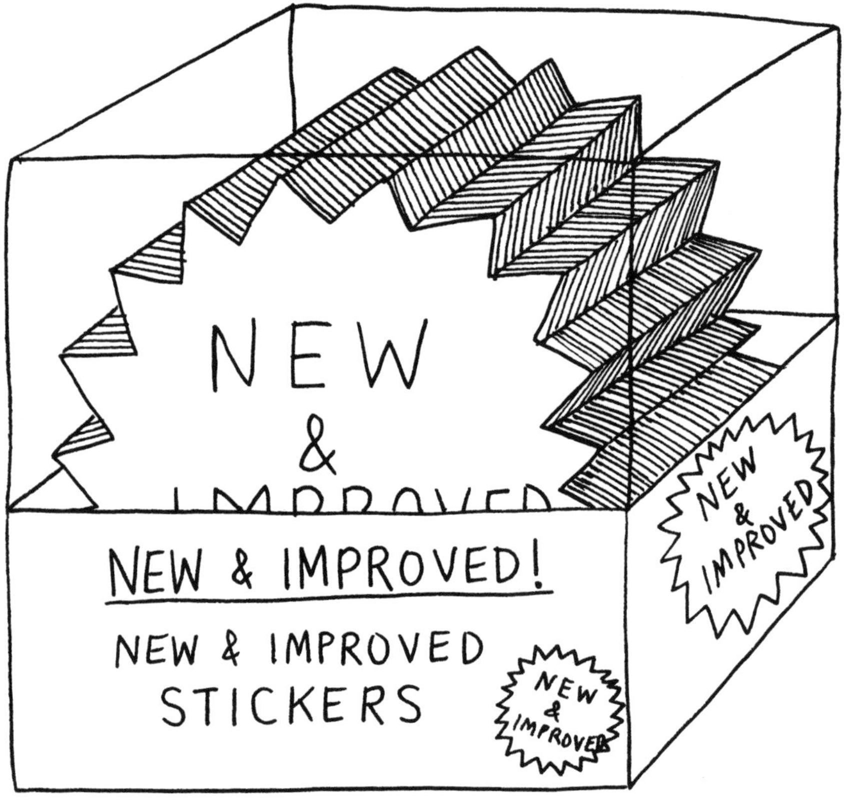
NEW
&
IMPROVED
NEW & IMPROVED!
NEW & IMPROVED
STICKERS
NEW
&
IMPROVED
NEW
&
IMPROVED

LIFE

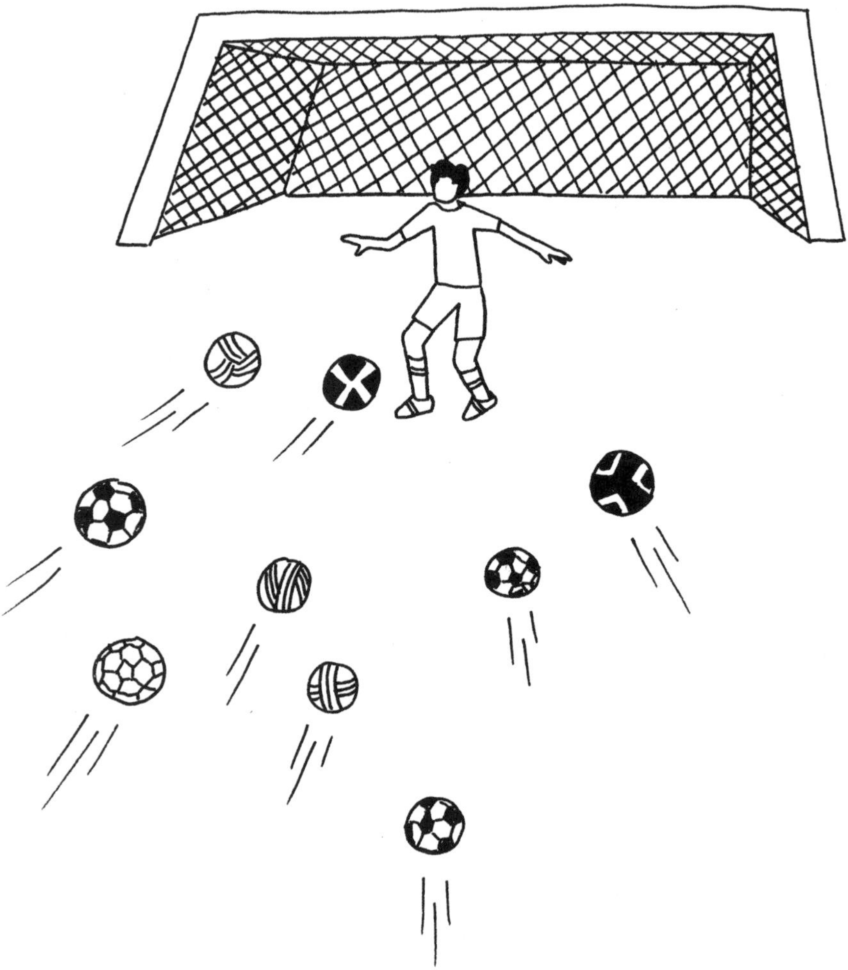

"Mine work but I can't fly. They told me I was barely good enough to get into Heaven, so I should just be happy to be here. And you know, they do keep flies away."

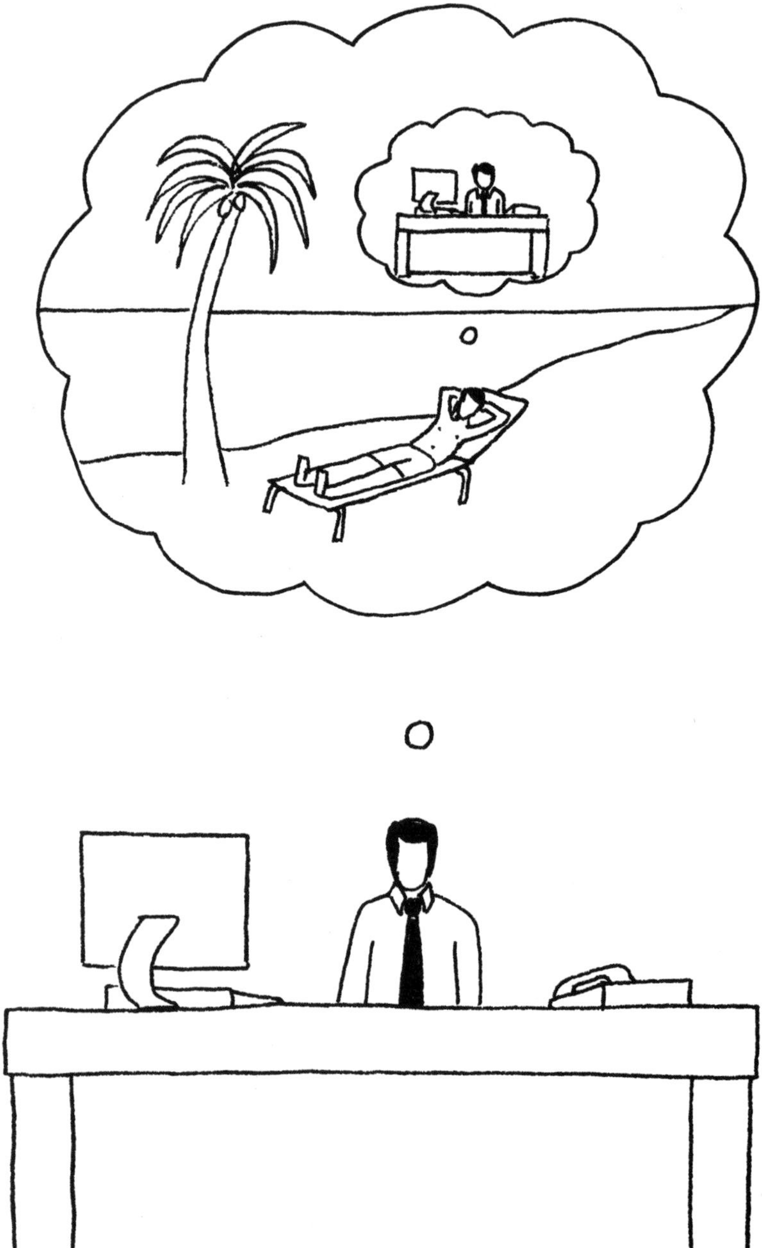

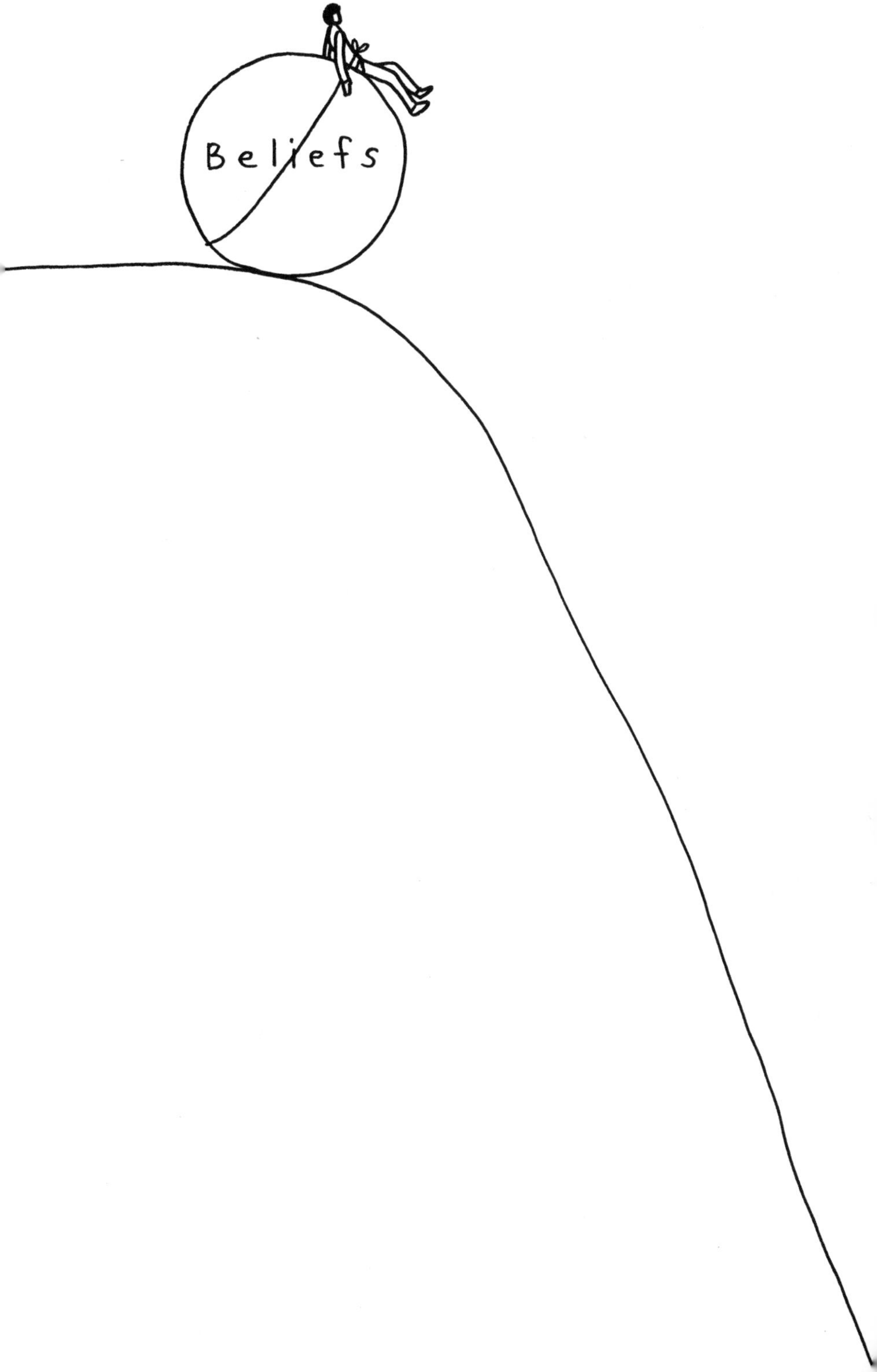
Beliefs

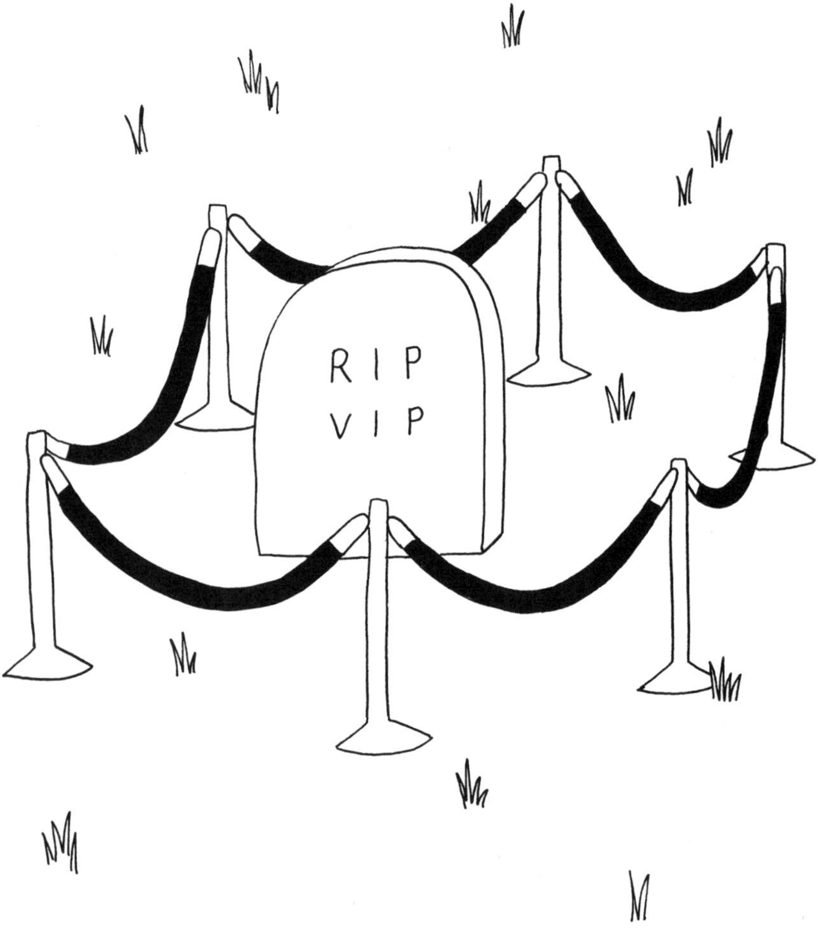
RIP
VIP

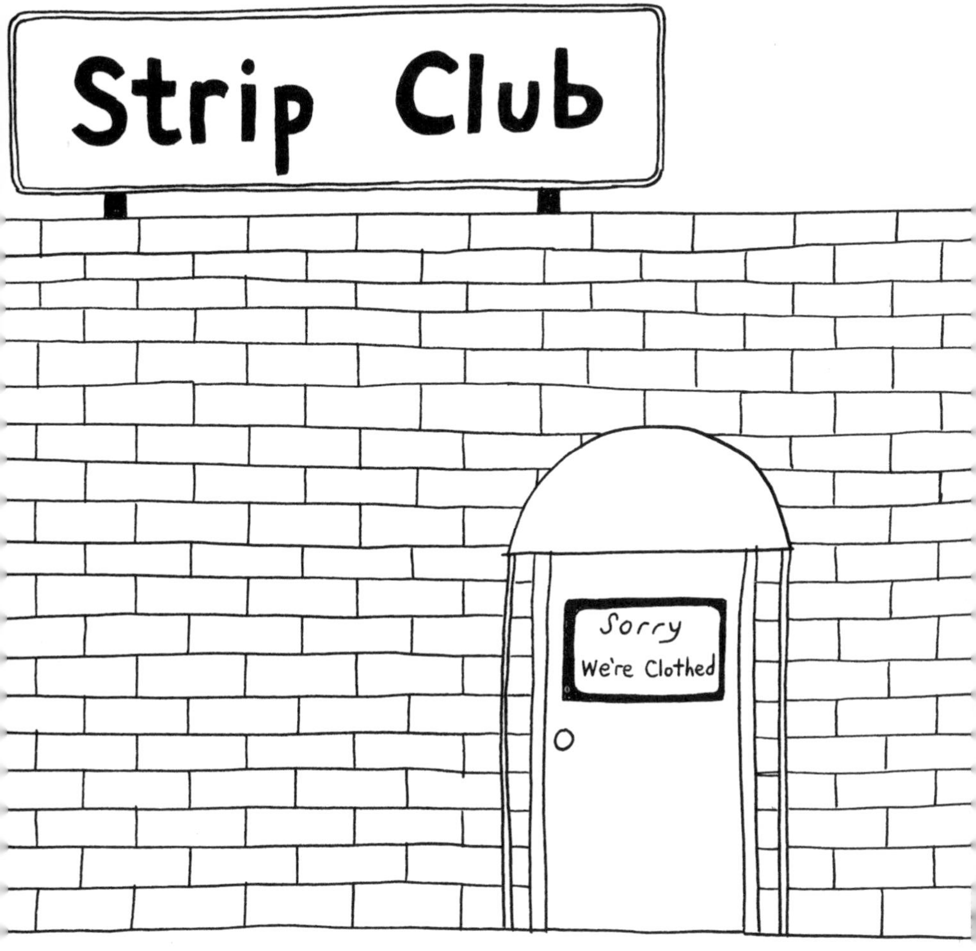
Strip Club
Sorry
We're Clothed

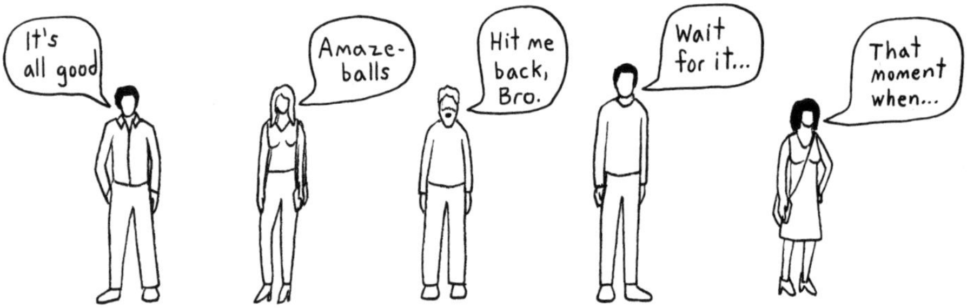
It's all good
Amaze-balls
Hit me back, Bro.
Wait for it...
That moment when...

Choose Your Idiot

FRONT

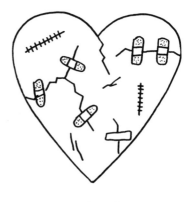

BACK

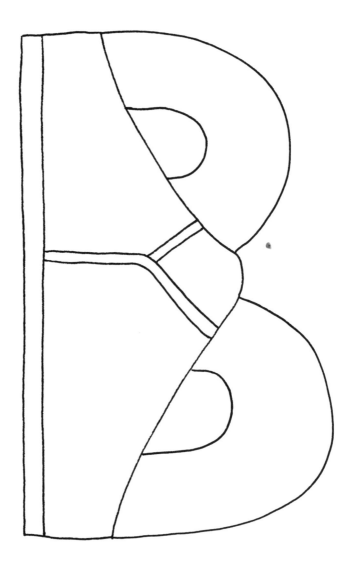

B Wearing Underwear

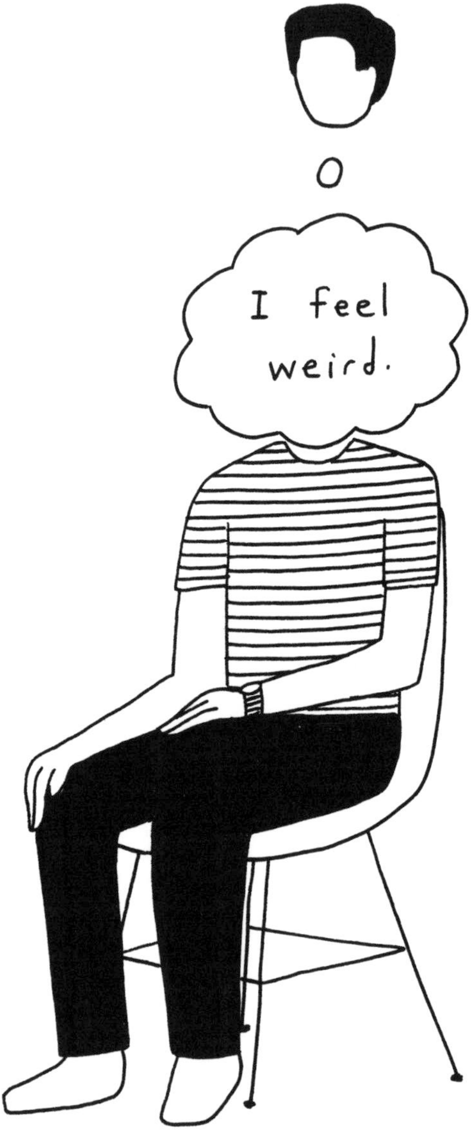
I feel weird.

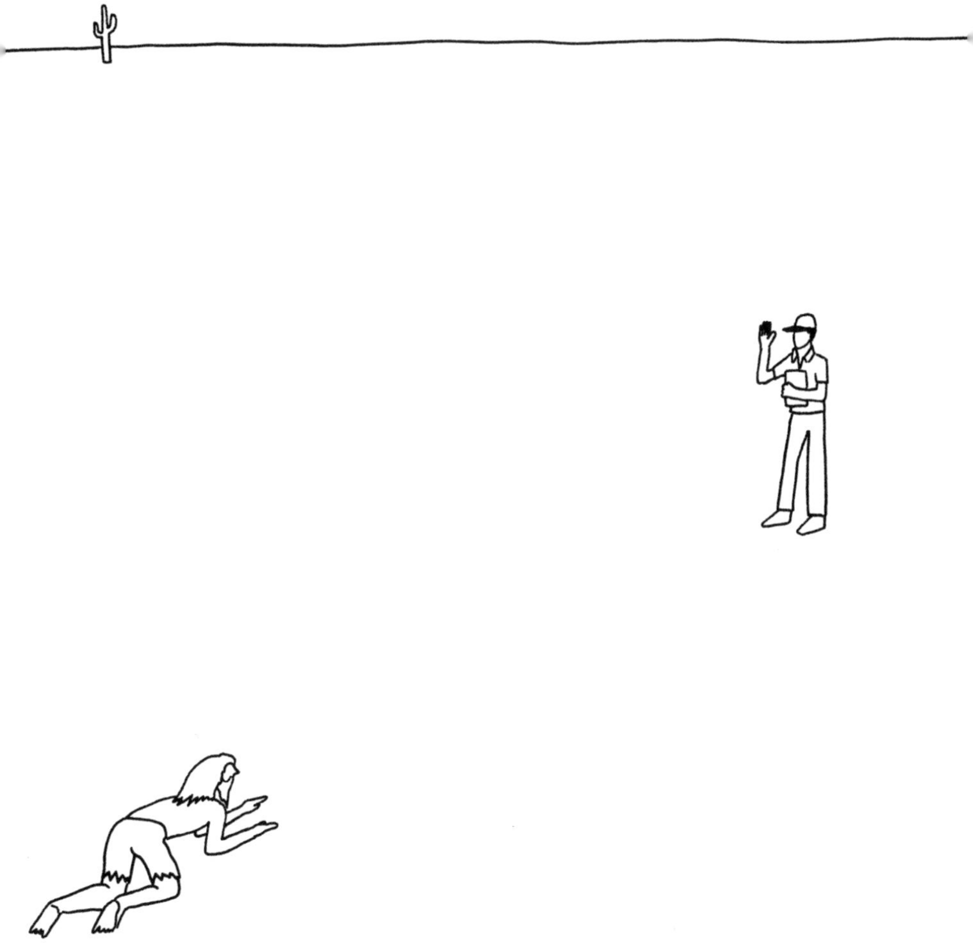

"Hey there! Got a minute for the environment?"

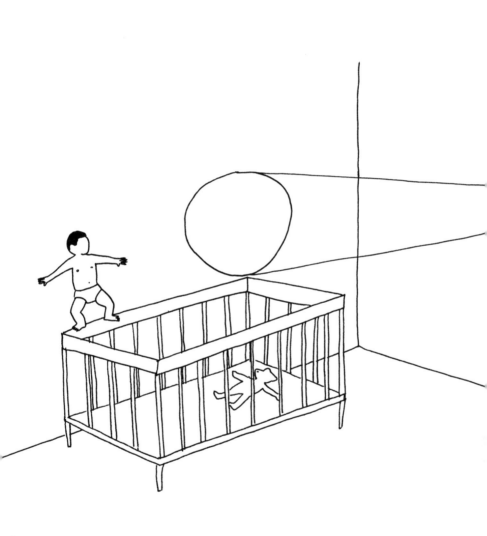

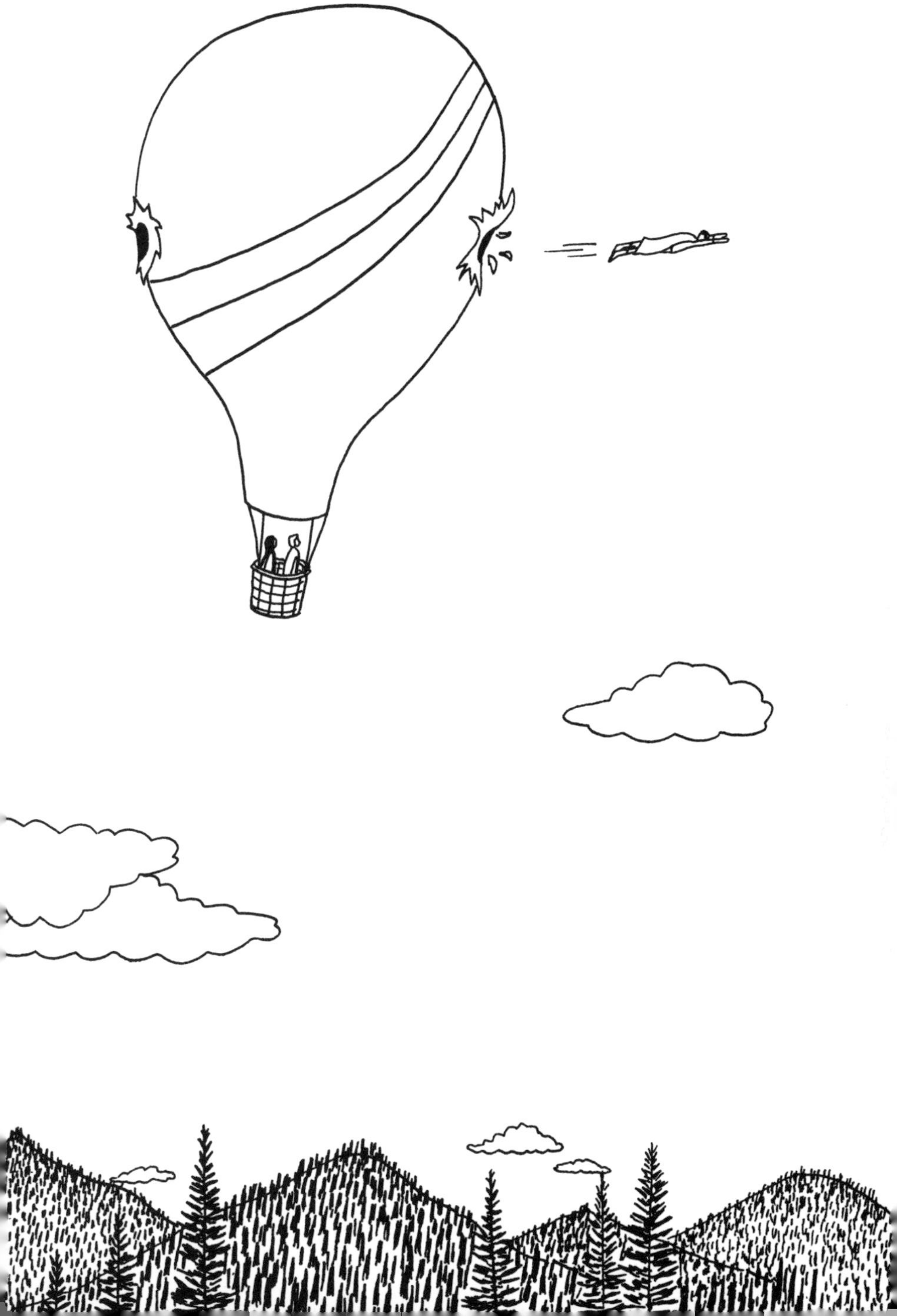

Venn Diagram

Tough Guys
Spandex

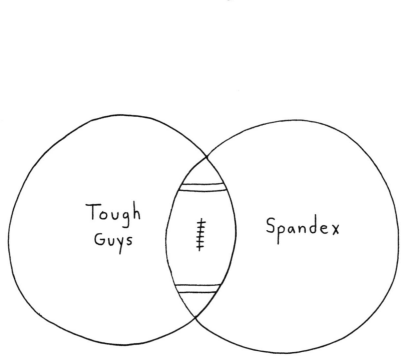

Witch Cleaning Up

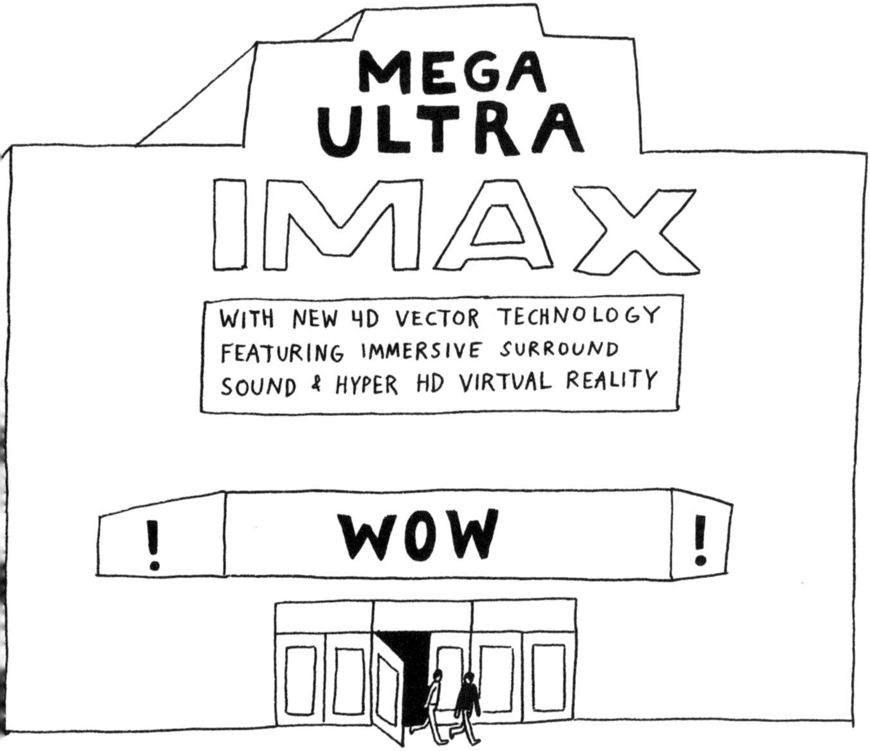
MEGA
ULTRA
IMAX
WITH NEW 4D VECTOR TECHNOLOGY FEATURING IMMERSIVE SURROUND SOUND & HYPER HD VIRTUAL REALITY
! WOW !

"Meh."

One-Man Band

One-Man Band's
Groupies

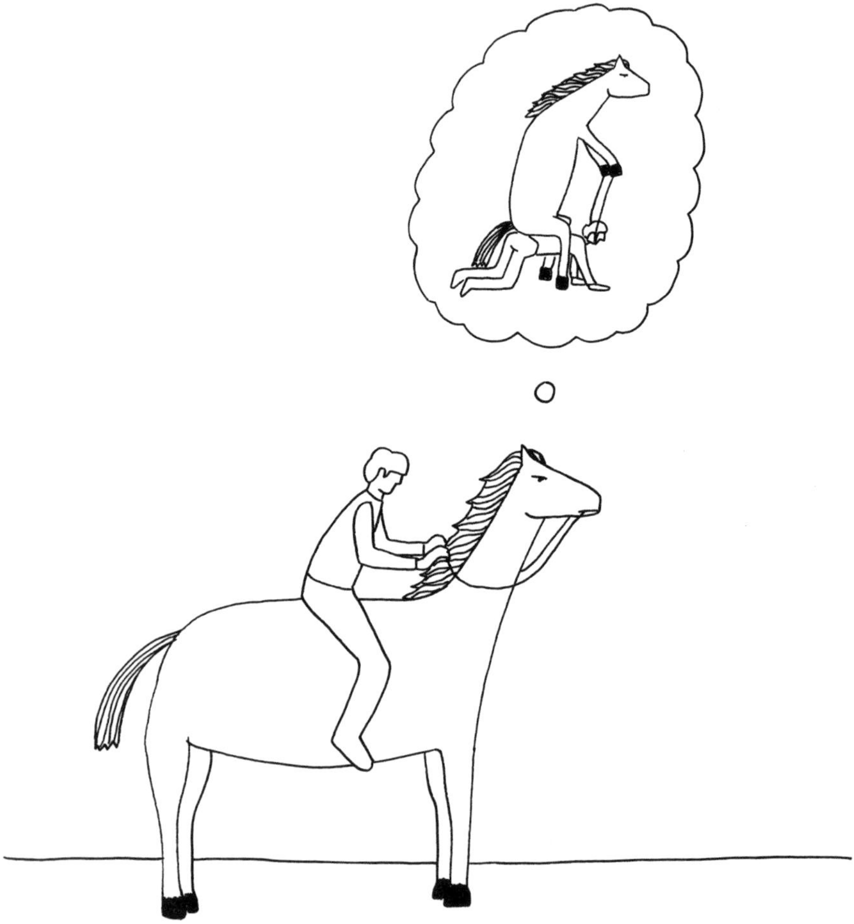

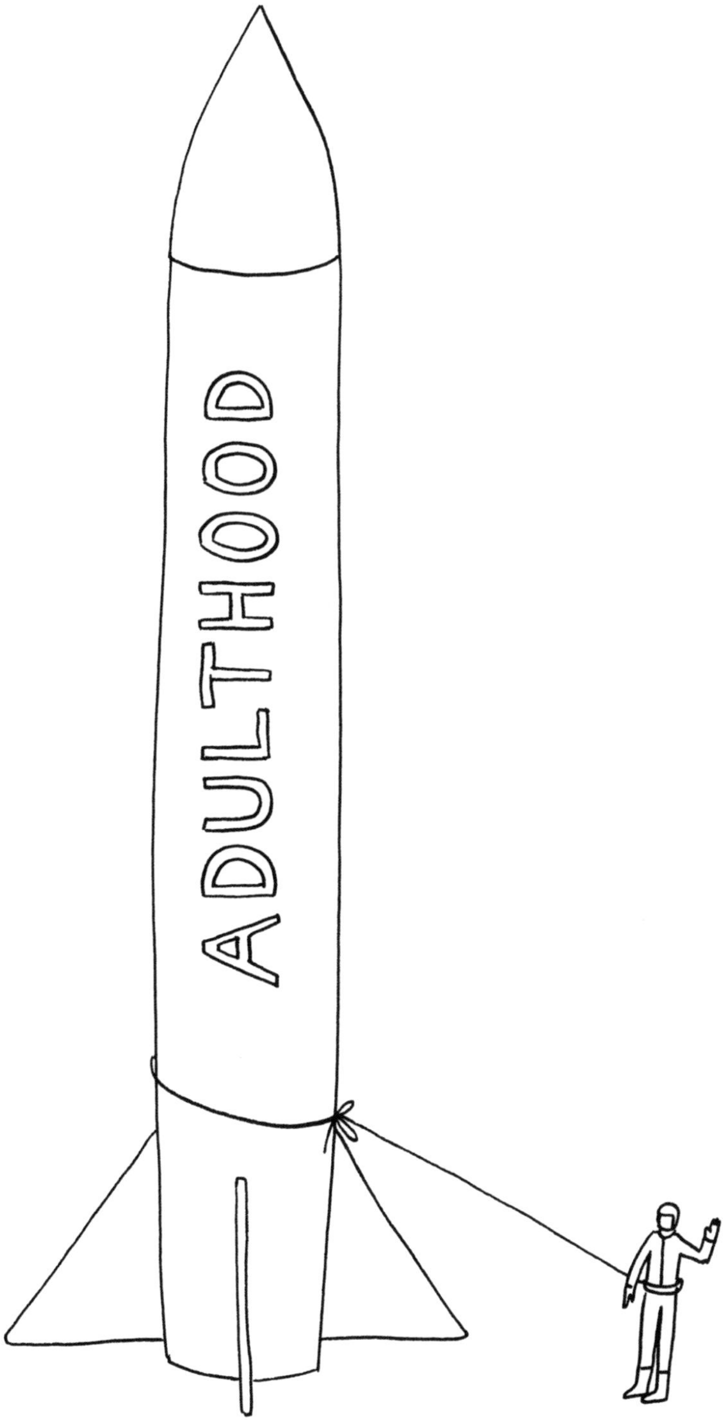
ADULTHOOD

Matt remembers his disagreement
with witch doctor

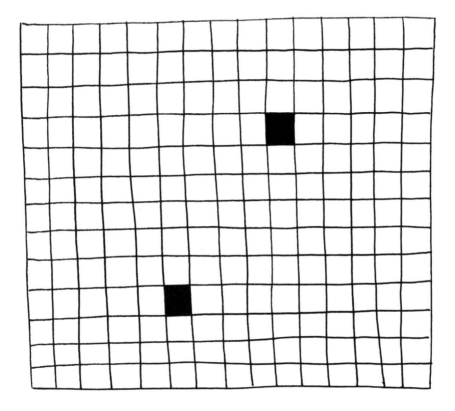

Really Hard Crossword Puzzle

Future Ex-friends

sculptor

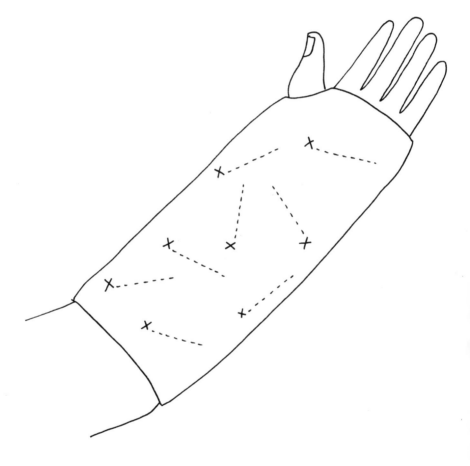

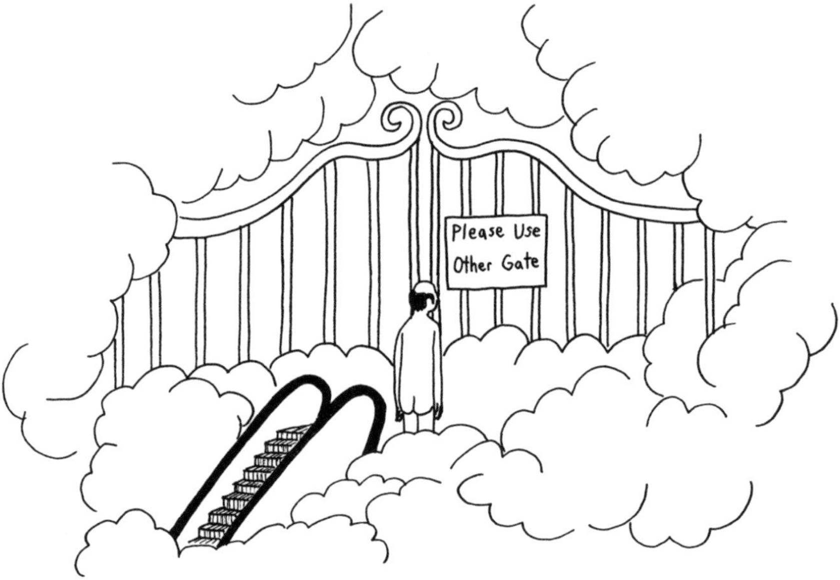
Please Use
Other Gate

Turtle with Helmet

Get a room.

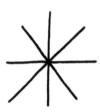

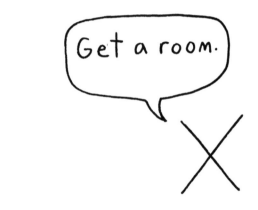

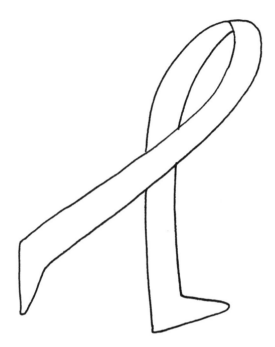

Ribbon Worn in Support of Legs

Tiger	Breakfast Cereal
Camel	Cigarettes
Lion	Movie Studio
Bear	Football Team
Cheetah	Junk Food
Eagle	Country
Weasel	Still Available

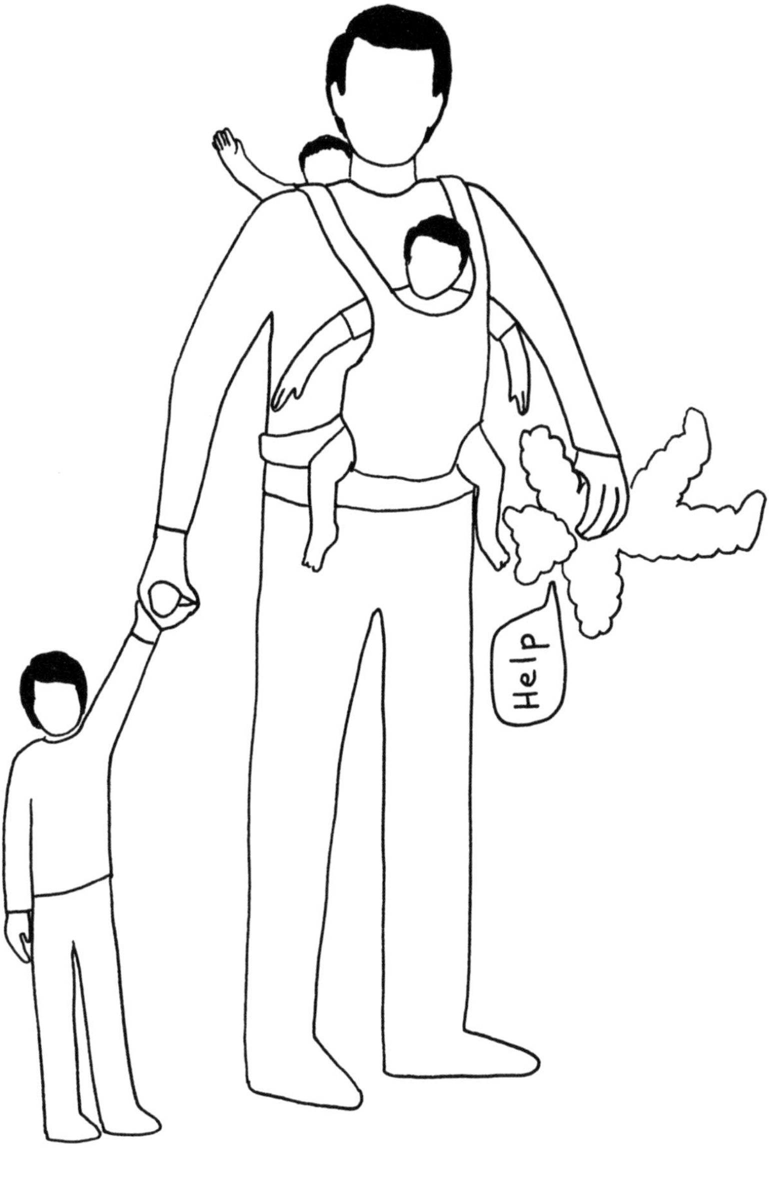
Help

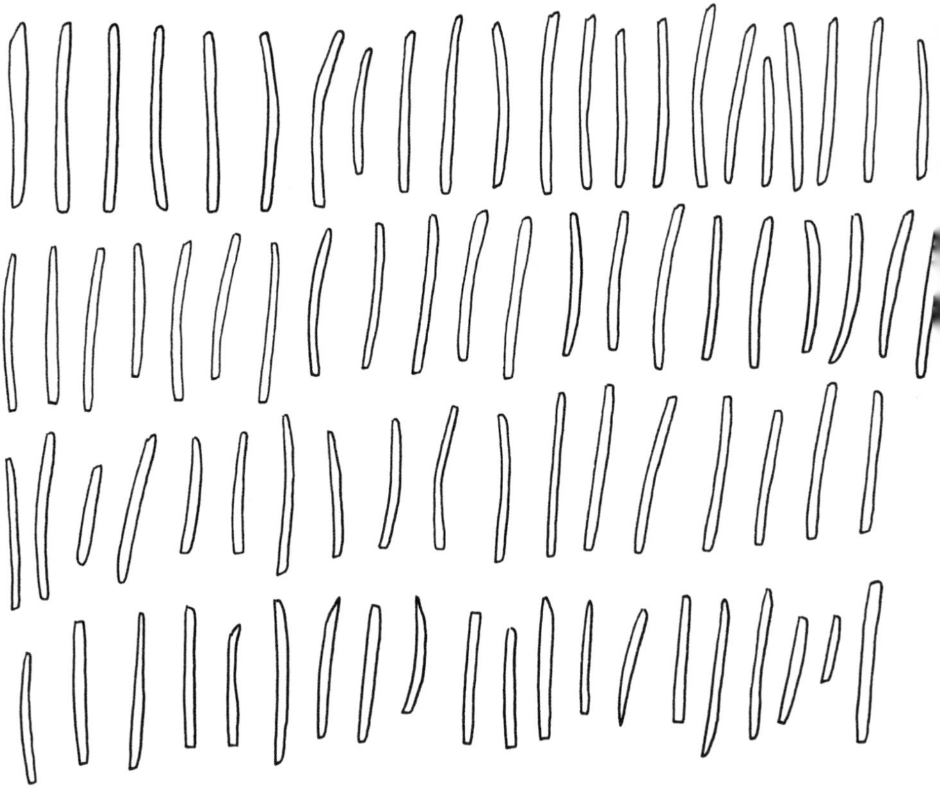

All of the French Fries You Just Ate

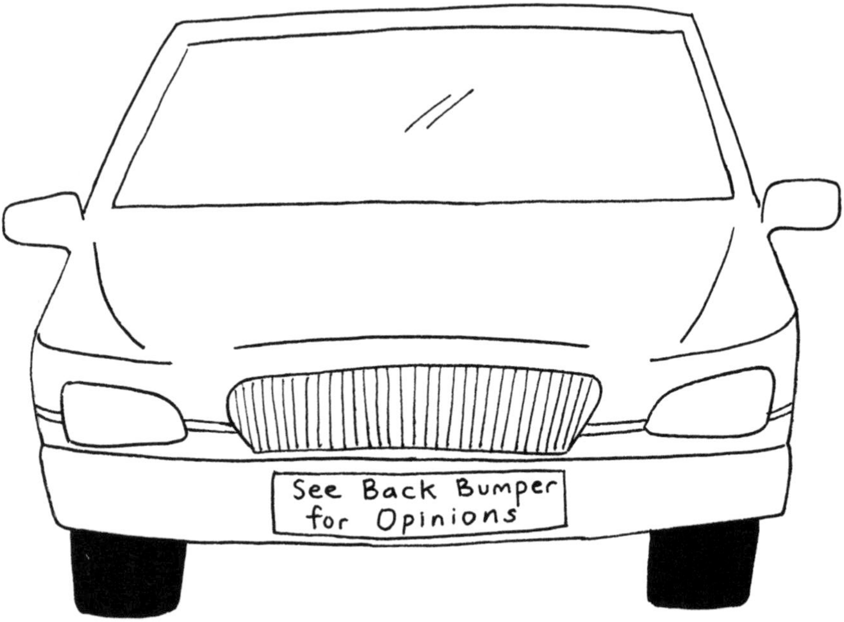
See Back Bumper
for Opinions

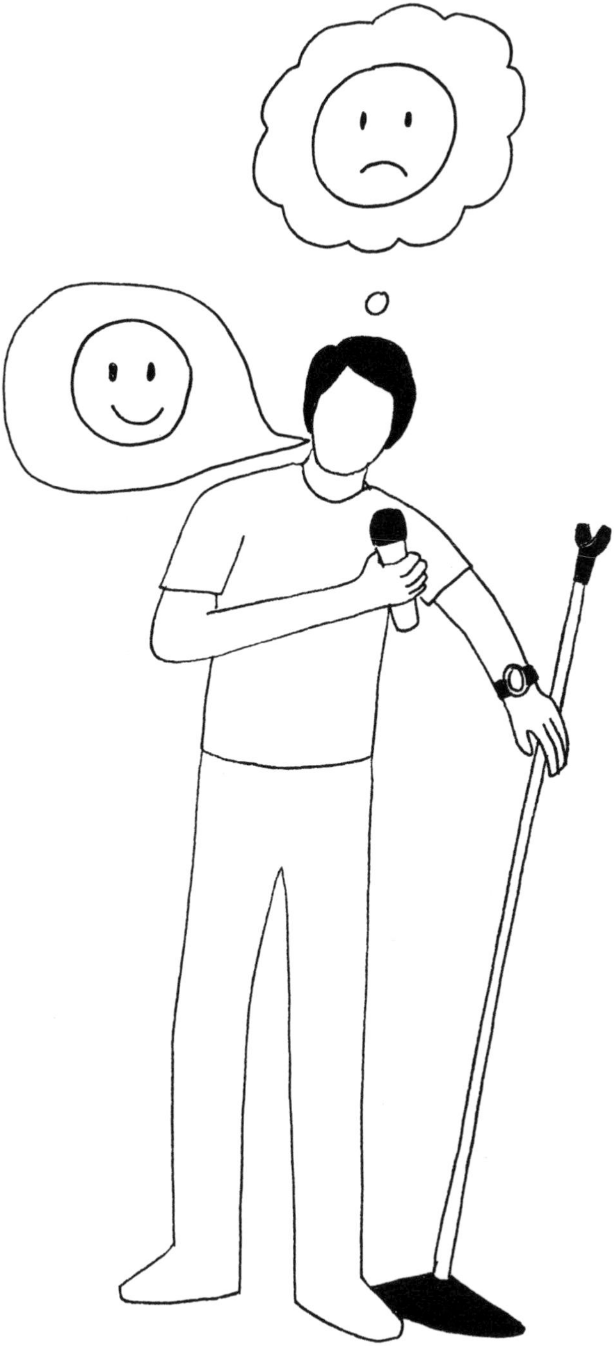

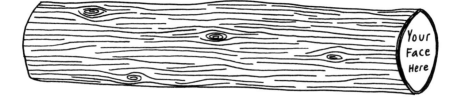

Your
Face
Here

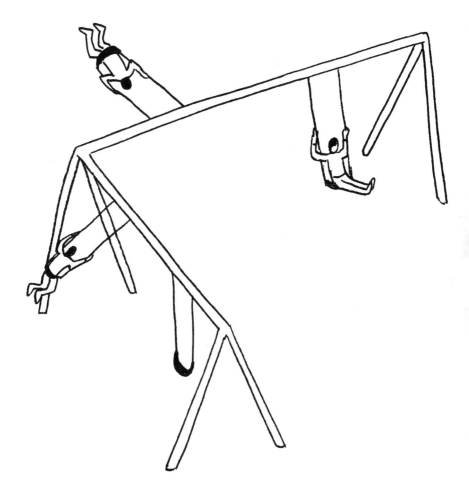

Failed Ice Cream Flavors

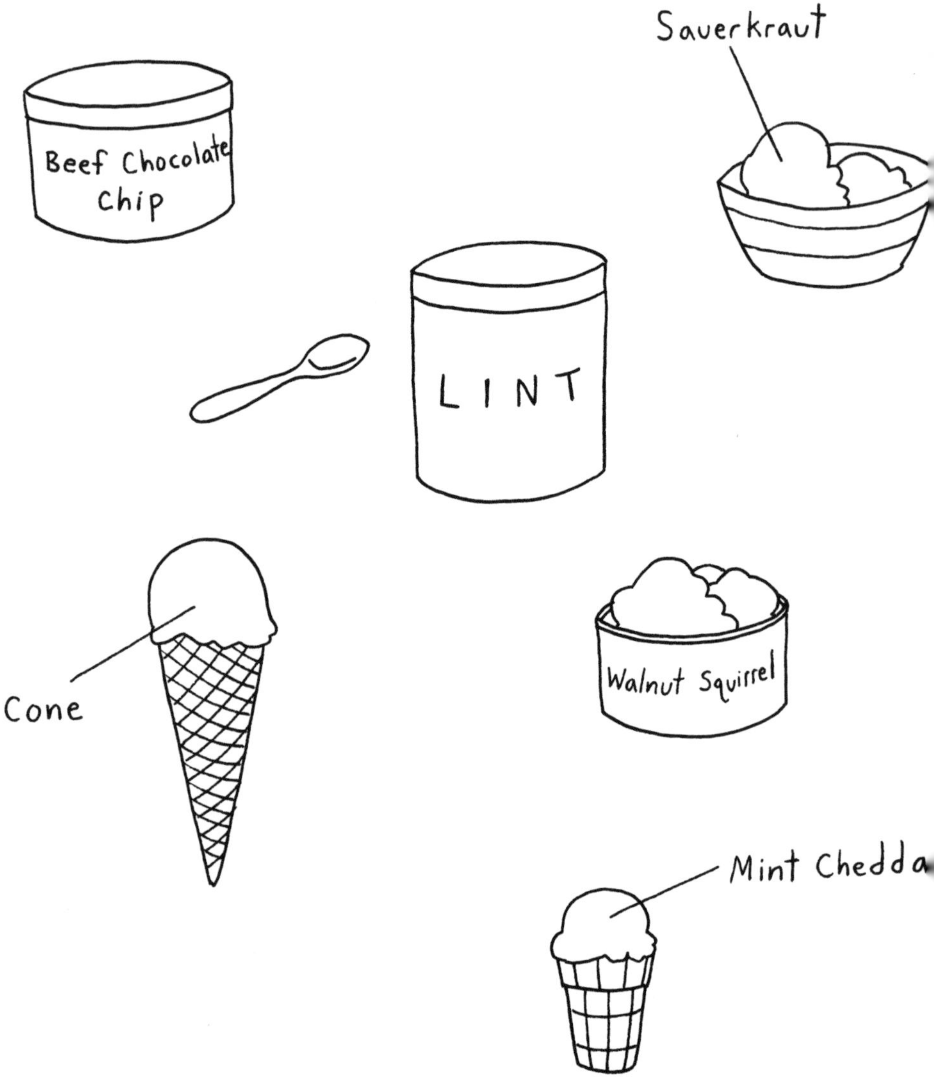
Sauerkraut
Beef Chocolate Chip
LINT
Walnut Squirrel
Cone
Mint Chedda

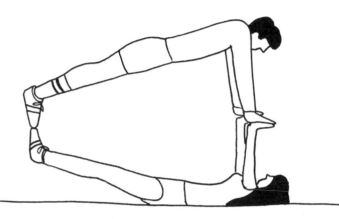

Athletic Couple Doing Foreplay

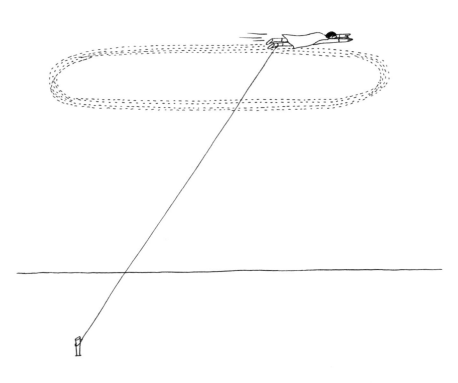

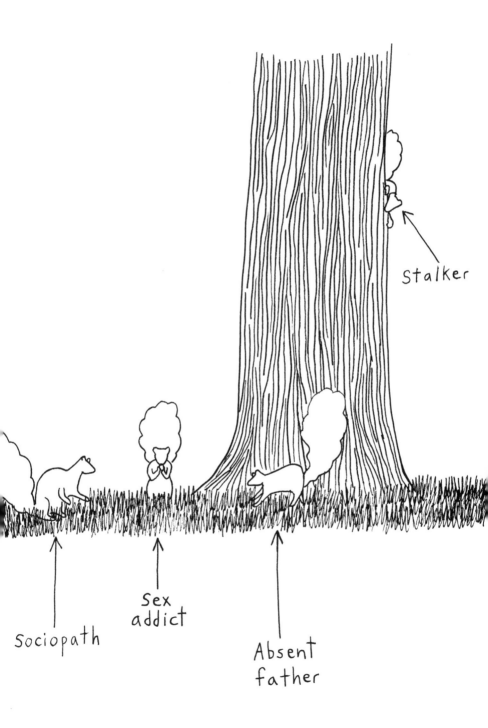

Stalker

Sociopath

Sex
addict

Absent
father

Skull and Crossbones
(when he was still alive)

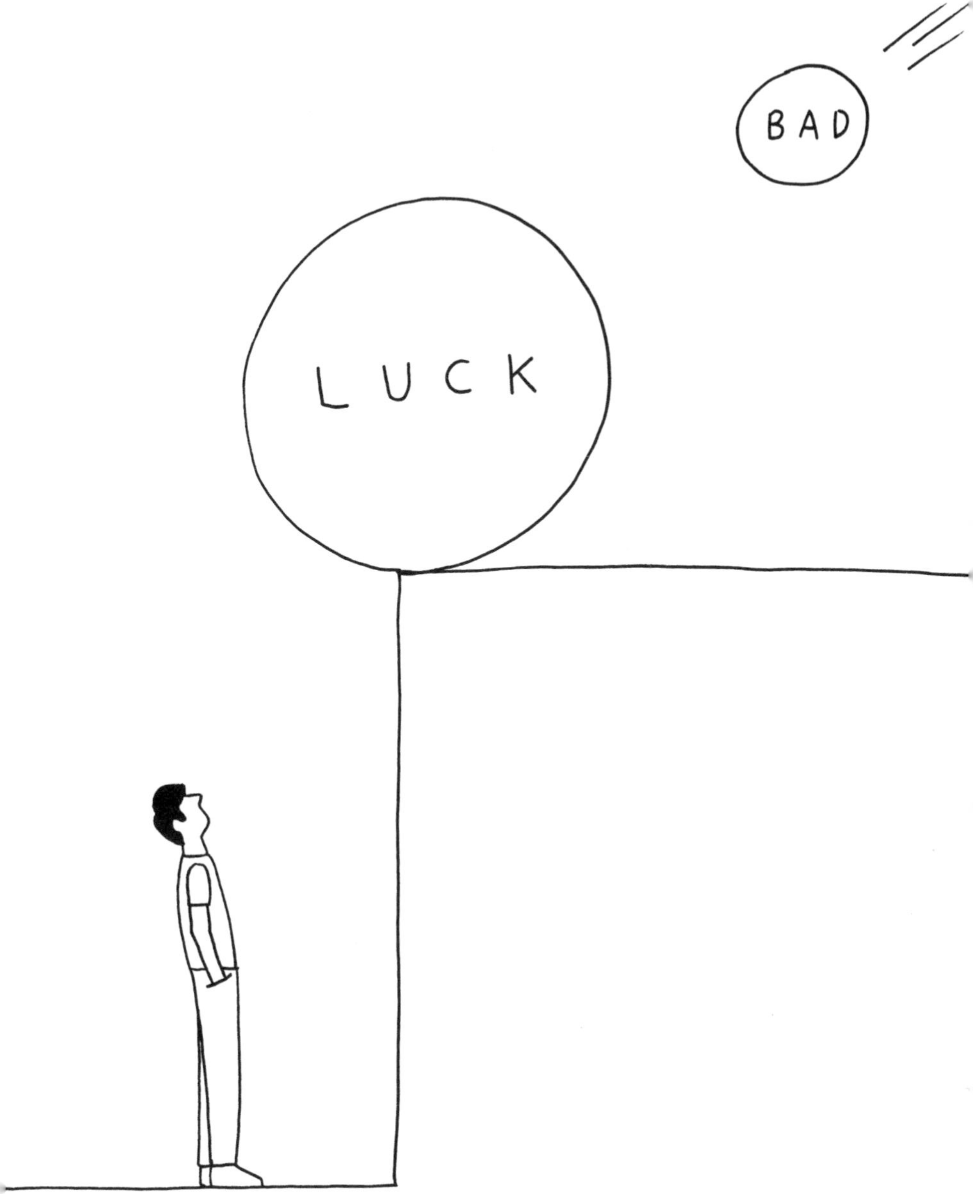
BAD
LUCK

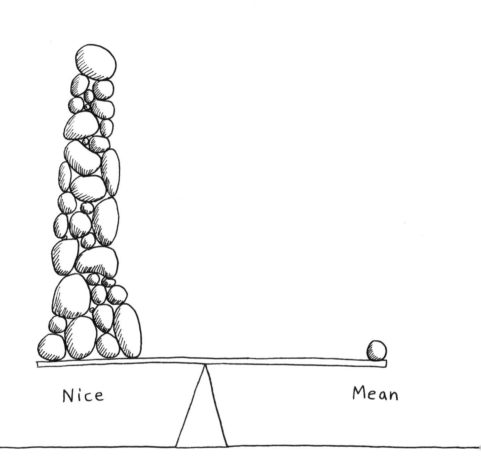

Nice

Mean

COMMENTS

Period
Too
Fore
To
Sicks
Ellipsis

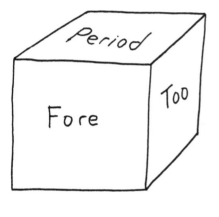

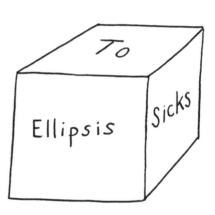

"The Fart"

Ideas for Band Photo

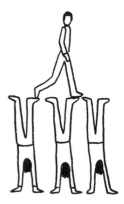

Pimp in Quicksand

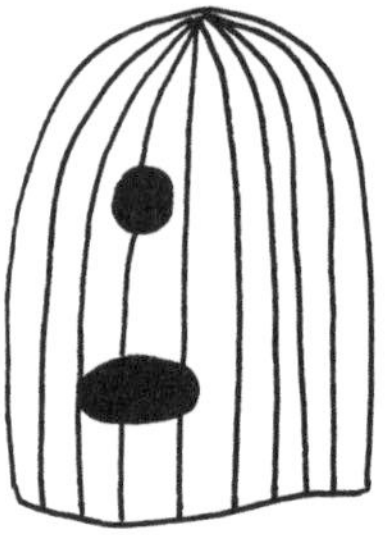

Hat Belongs to
Cyclops Burglar

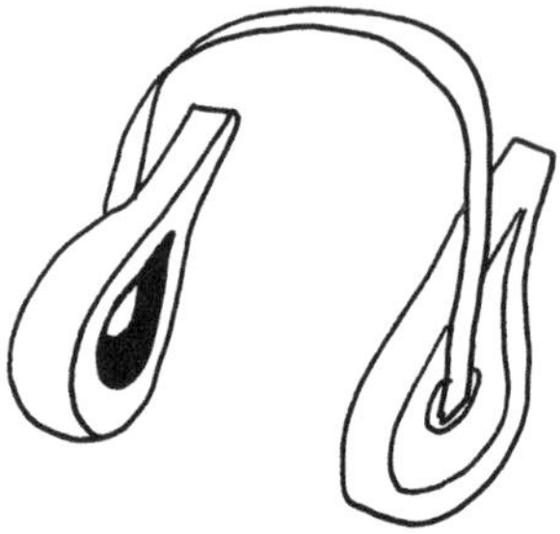

Earmuffs Belong to
Elf Baggage Handle

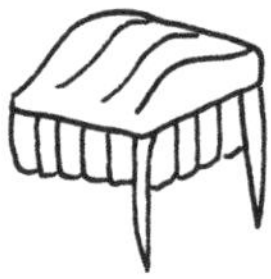

Dentures Belong to
Vampire Grandfather

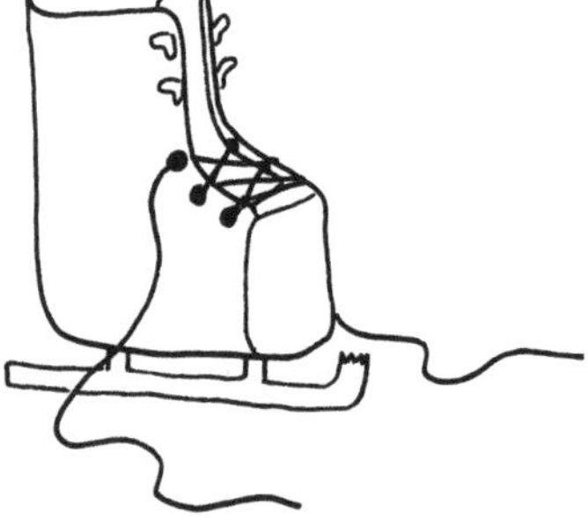

Skate Belongs to
Centaur Figure Skater

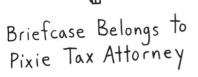

Briefcase Belongs to
Pixie Tax Attorney

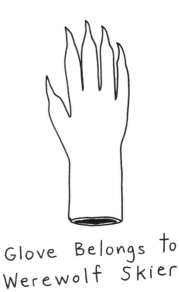

Glove Belongs to
Werewolf Skier

omputer Belongs to
roll Internet Troll

Headband*Belongs to
Ghost Pilates Instructor

*Invisible

CAT
HOUSE
OWNER
SMELL

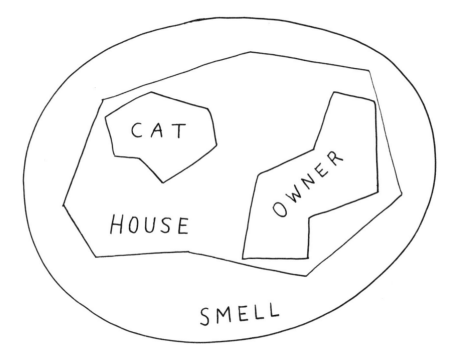

Jack vs. Bob

Jack	Bob
Jackrabbit	Bobcat
Jack Knife	Bobsled
Jack O'lantern	Bobby Socks
Jack Off	Bob for Apples
Carjack	Hair Bob
Jack of All Trades	Bob of Some Trades*

* Not Confirmed

RELIGION

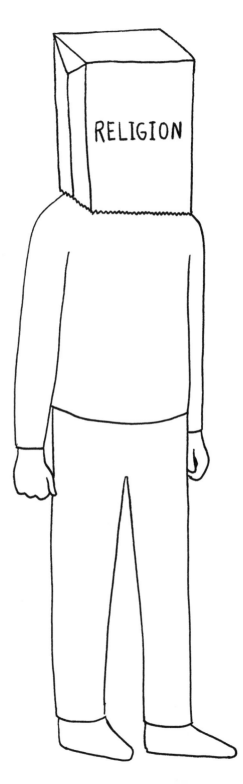

Diver gets into bed

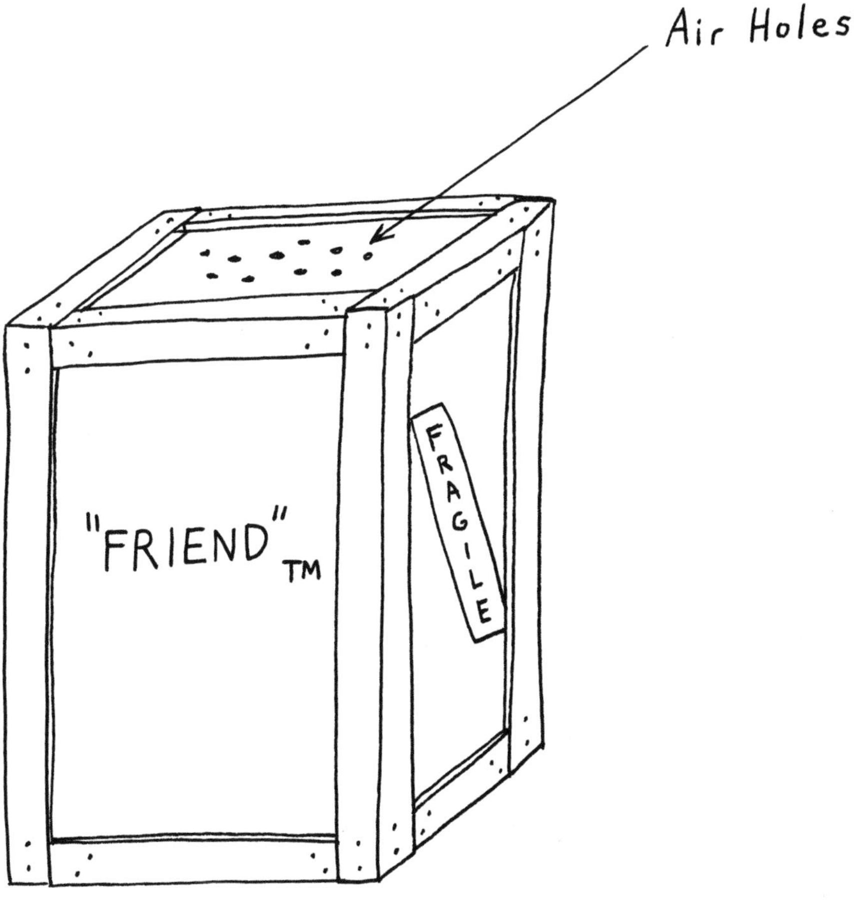
Air Holes
"FRIEND" TM
FRAGILE

"The good news is you're
still alive..."

American Flag

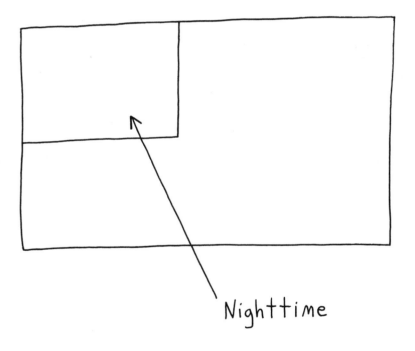

Nighttime

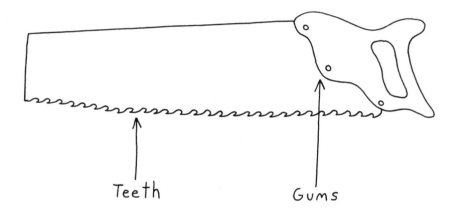

Teeth

Gums

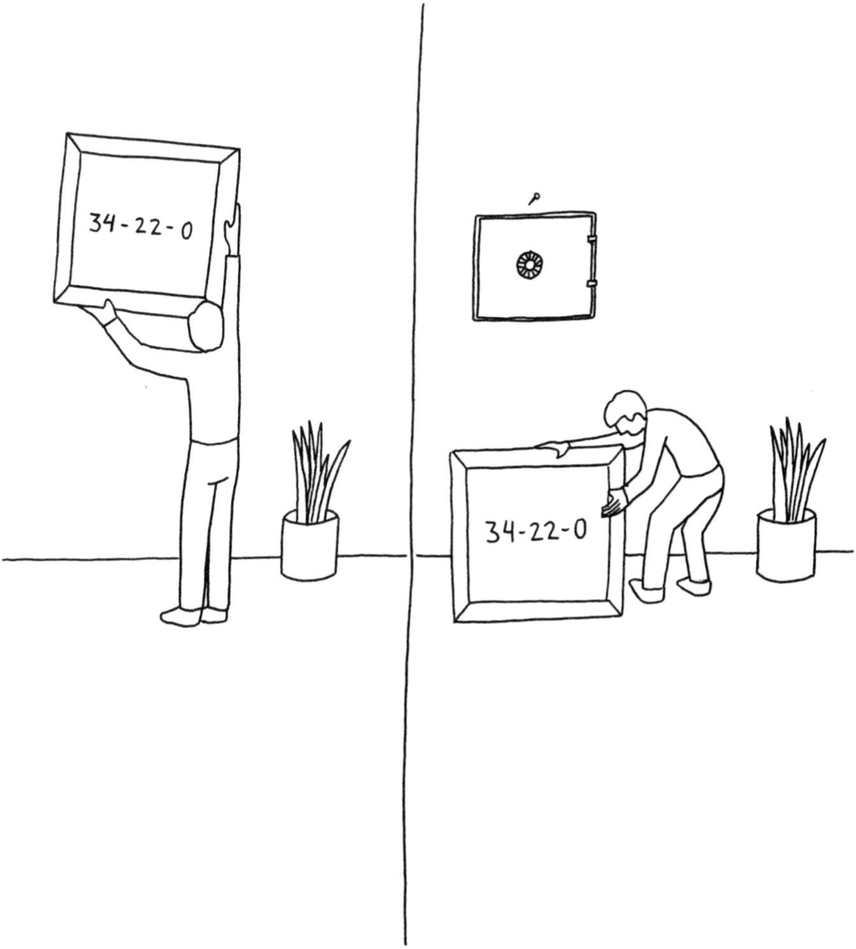
34-22-0
34-22-0

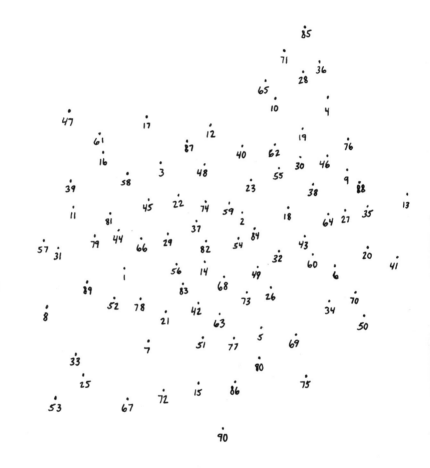

Scribble by Number

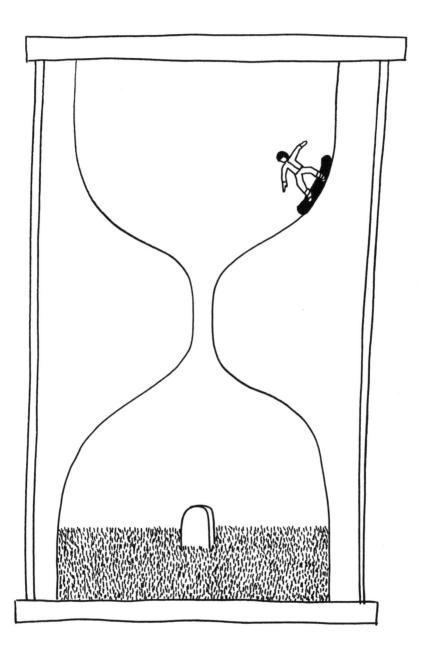

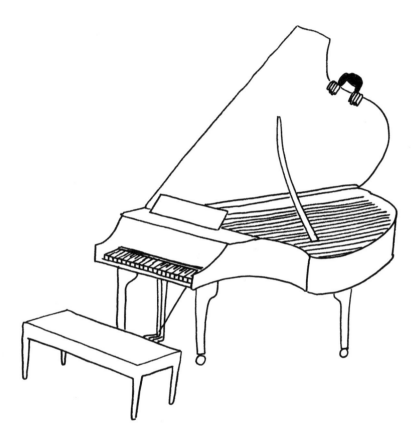

Piano player has lost his mind again

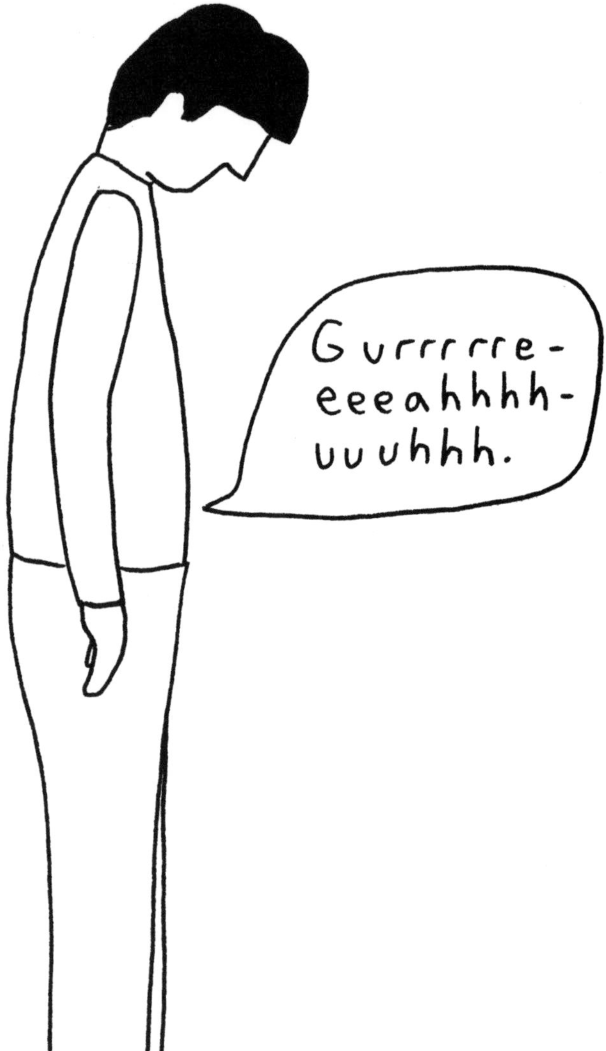
Gurrrrre-
eeeahhhh-
uuuhhh.

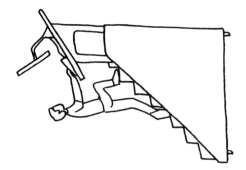

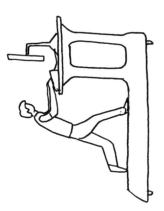

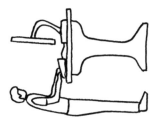

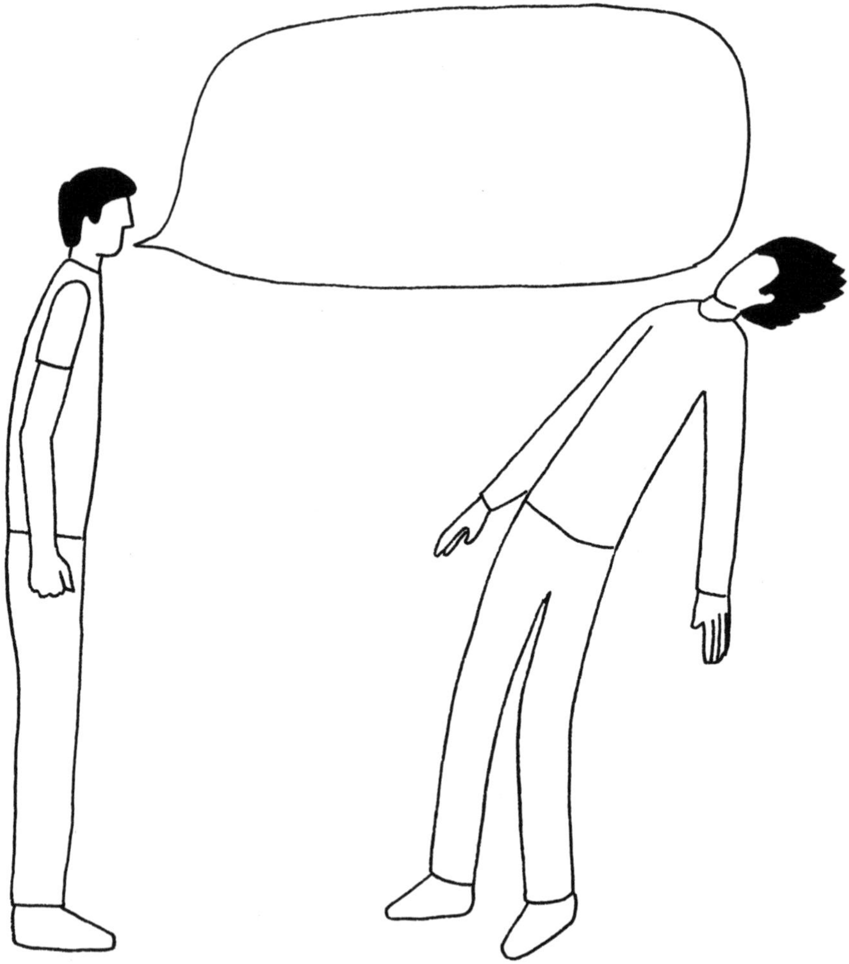

TO DO

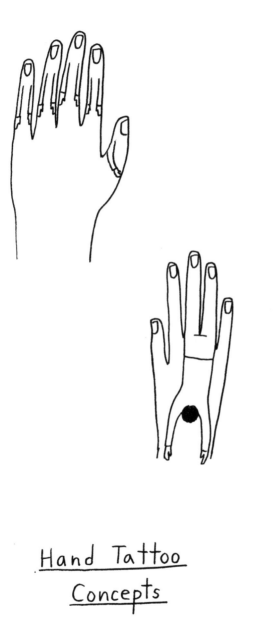

SEE
OTHER
HAND

Hand Tattoo
Concepts

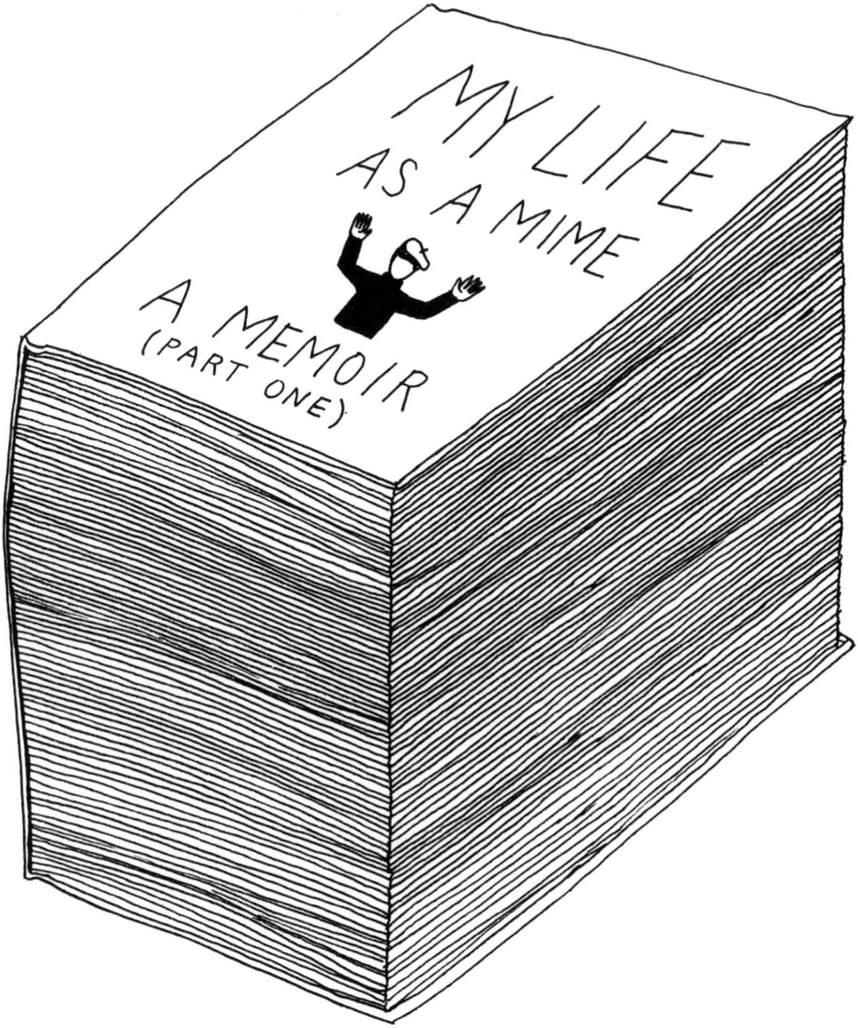

MY LIFE
AS A MIME
A MEMOIR
(PART ONE)

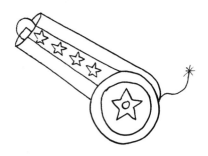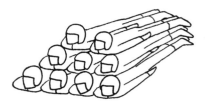

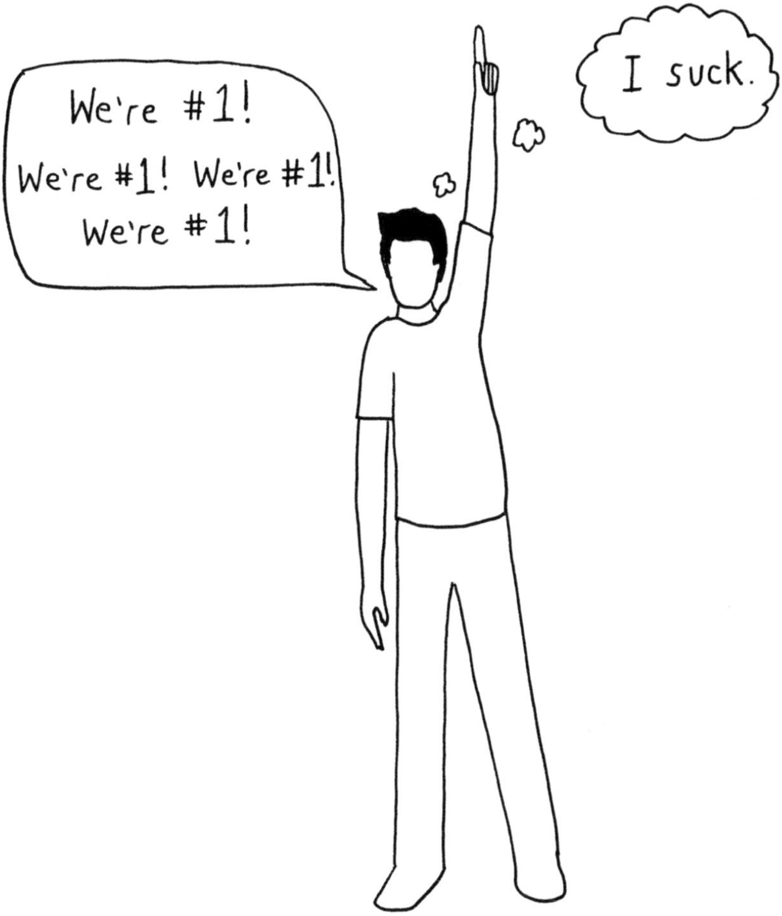
We're #1! We're #1! We're #1! We're #1!
I suck.

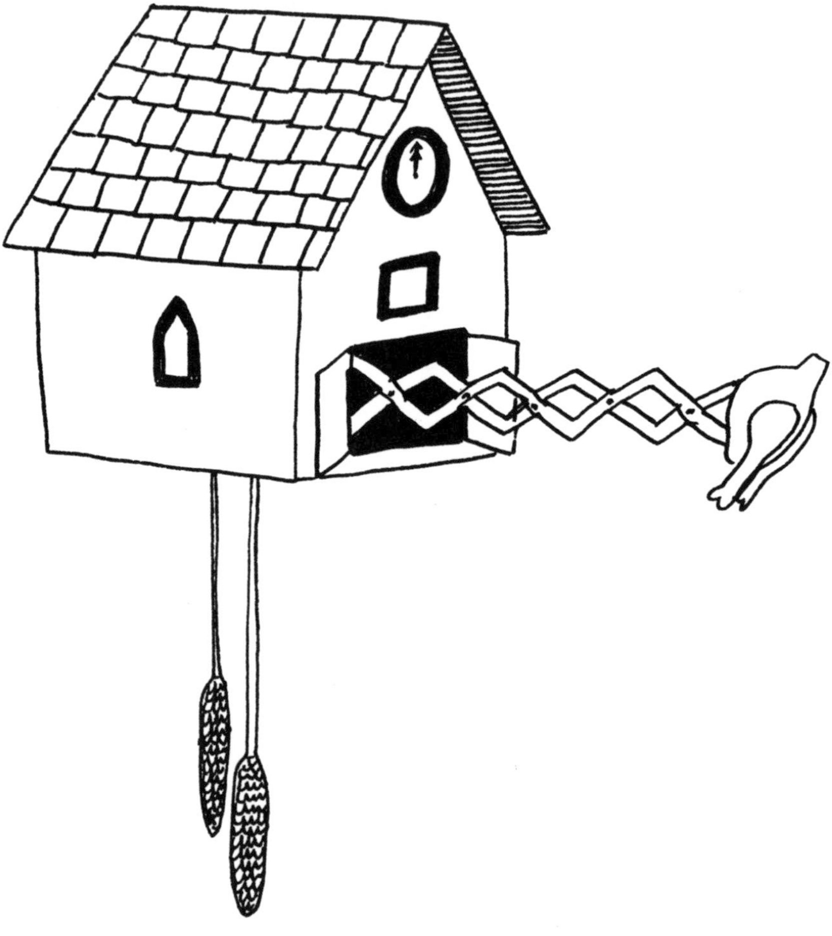

"Yeah, I agree. The powers are
great, but the 'helping people'
part gets old pretty fast."

Bobsled

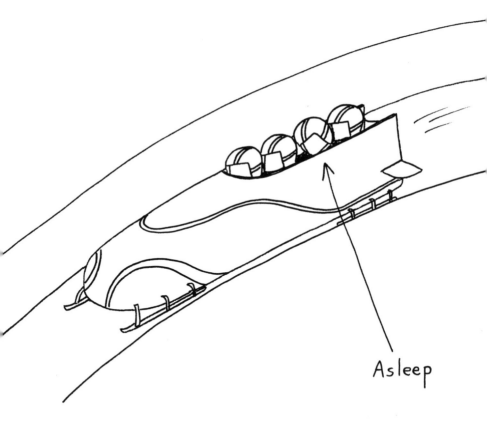

Asleep

H I

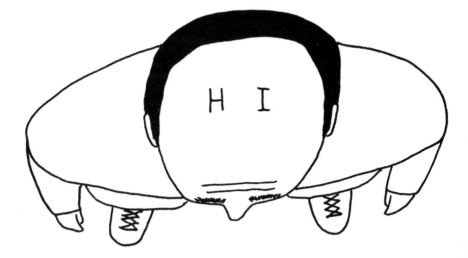

Head Tattoo

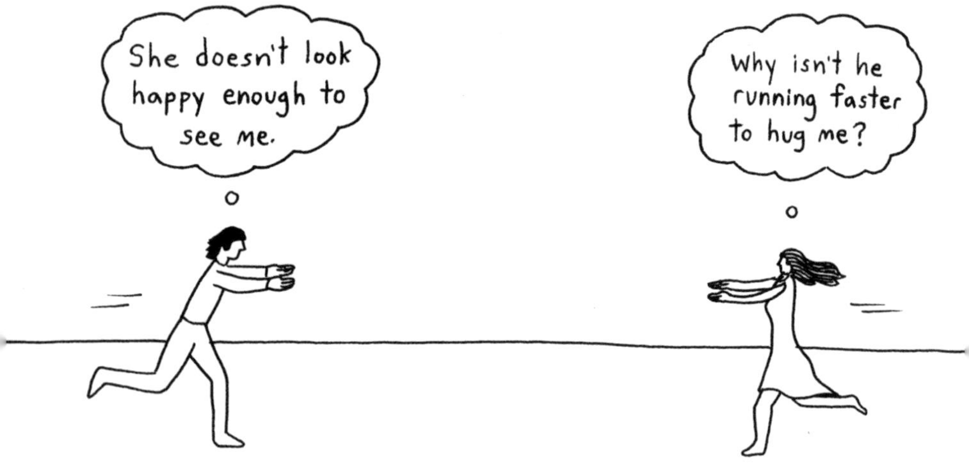
She doesn't look happy enough to see me.
Why isn't he running faster to hug me?

Platter

Head

As Per Last Will
and Testament

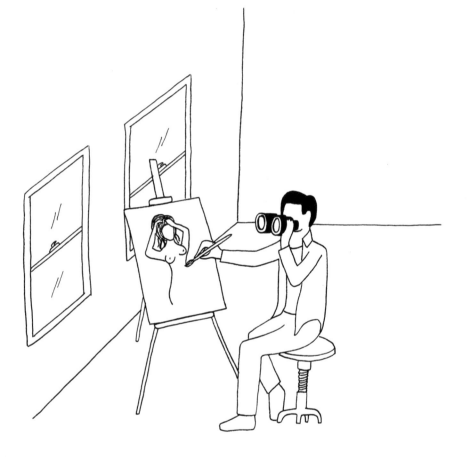

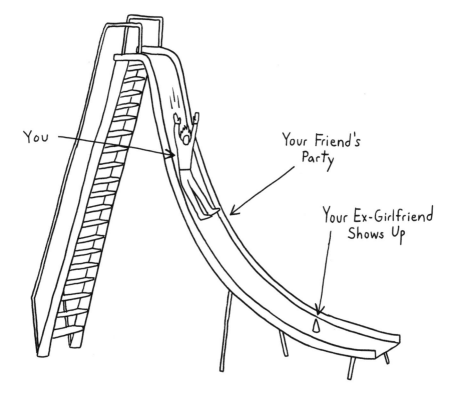

You

Your Friend's
Party

Your Ex-Girlfriend
Shows Up

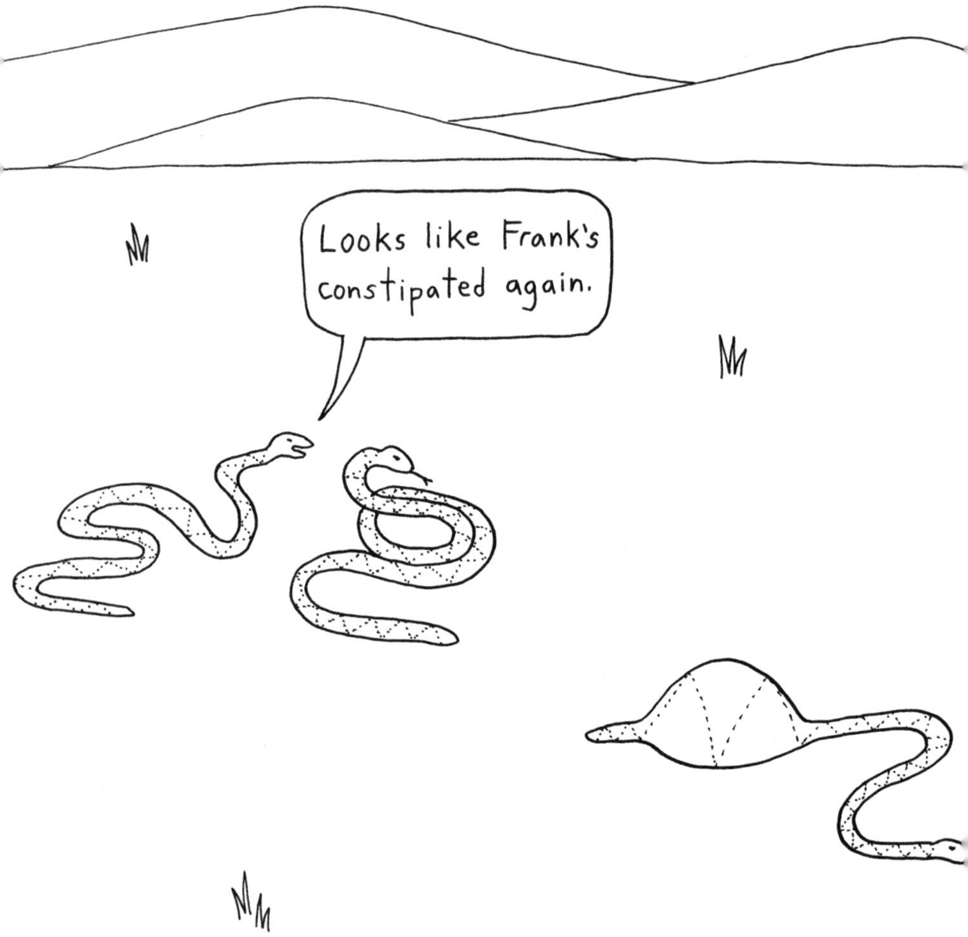
Looks like Frank's constipated again.

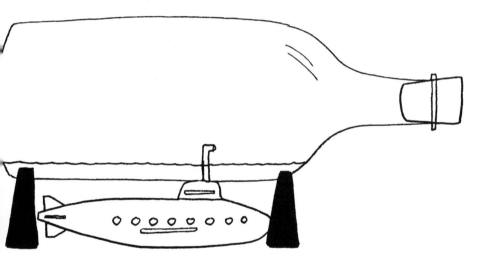

<u>Sports That Can Be Played</u>
<u>with Human Head</u>

1. Soccer

2. Volleyball

3. Bowling

4. Kickball

5. Water Polo

6. Tetherball

7. Golf *

* Just the eyes

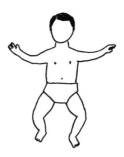

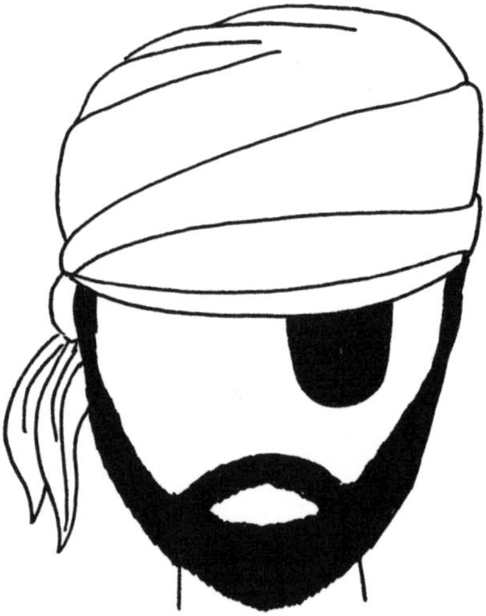

Pirate

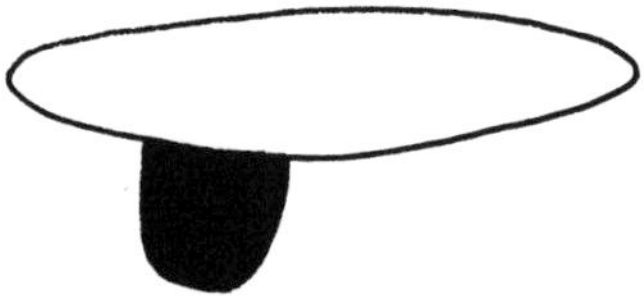

Pirate's
Sleep Mask

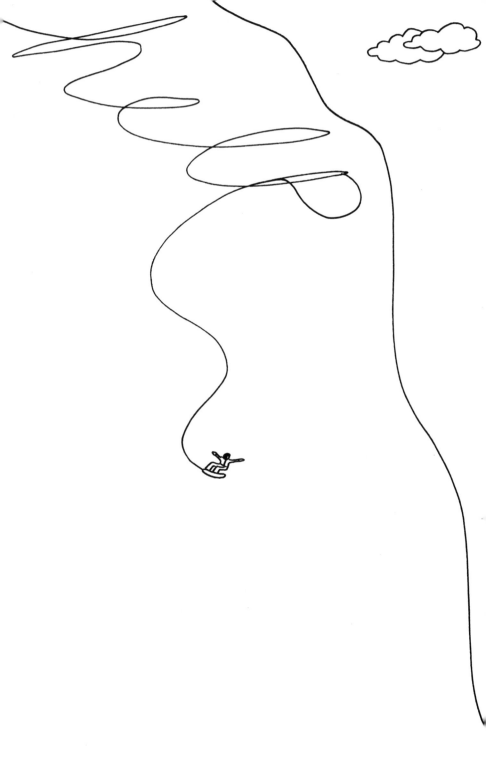

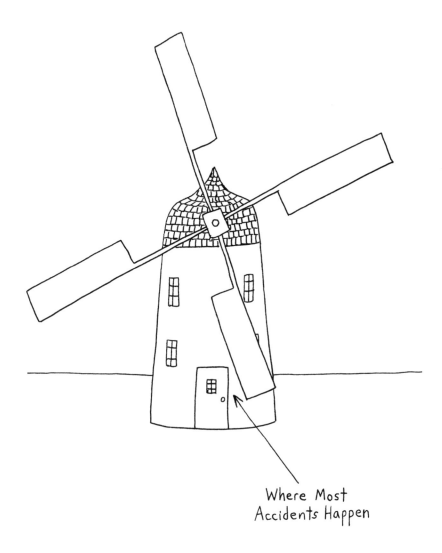

Where Most
Accidents Happen

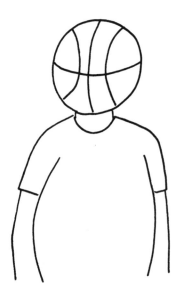

Americans

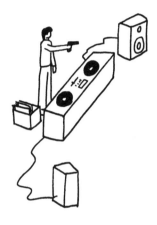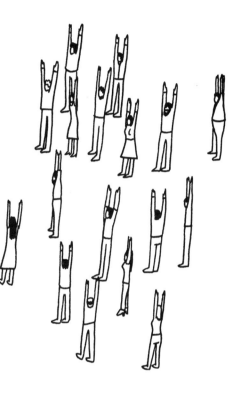

"...Now wave 'em like you just don't care."

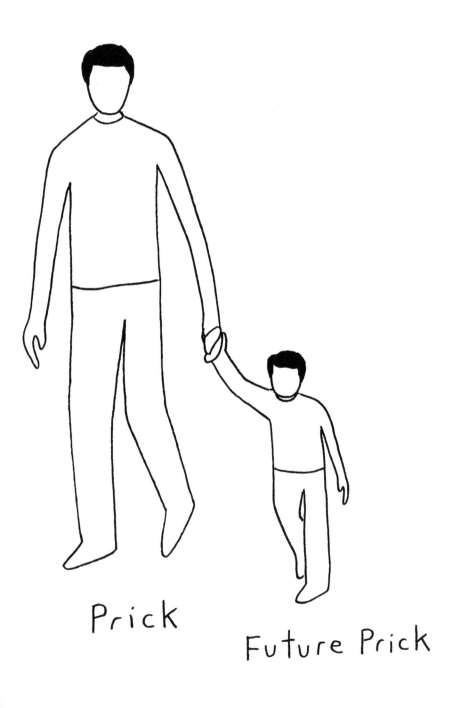

Prick

Future Prick

No

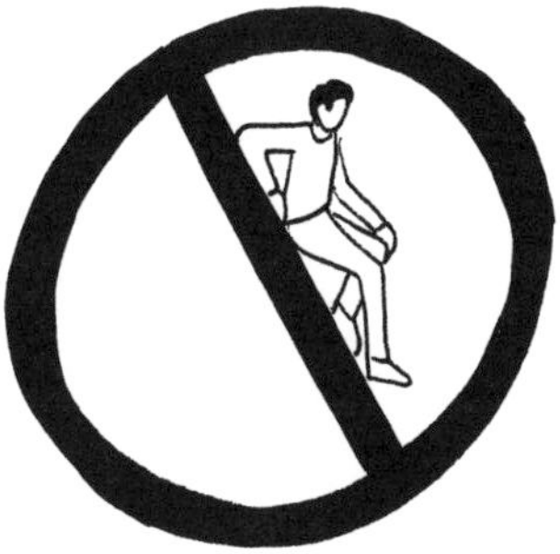

Relaxing on "No" Symbol

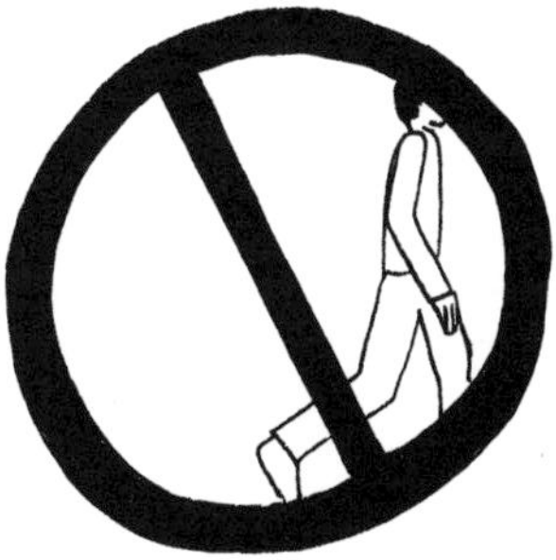

Leaving

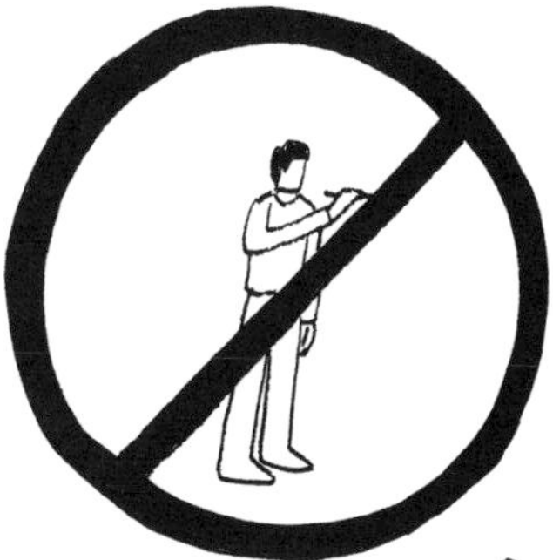

Prohibiting Yourself

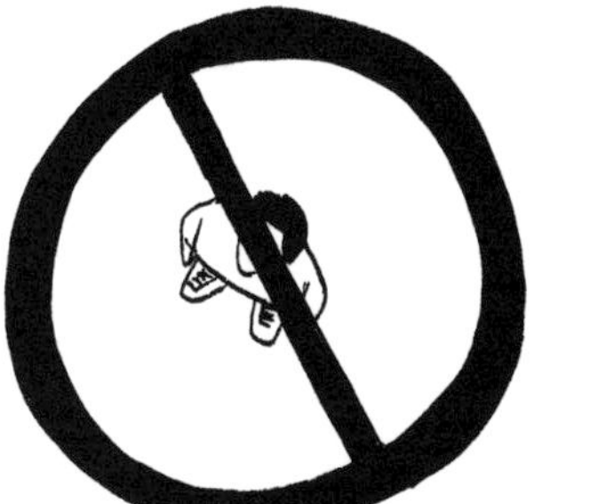

Looking up at "God"

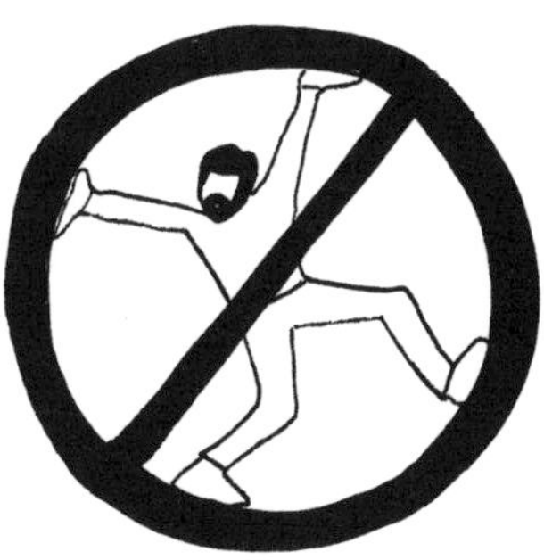

Rolling the Symbol

Golf ⟶ Mini Golf

Tennis ⟶ Table Tennis

Hockey ⟶ Air Hockey

Soccer ⟶ Foosball

Weight Lifting ⟶ Lifting Very Small Weights

What kind of music do you like?
Whatever kind you like but their earlier stuff.
Well, I like their unreleased demos, so--
Yeah, but I like the stuff they never even recorded.
Me too.

RIP

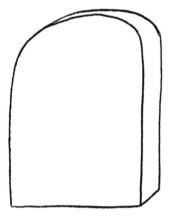

Human

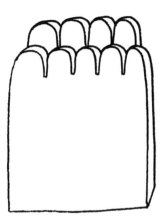

cat

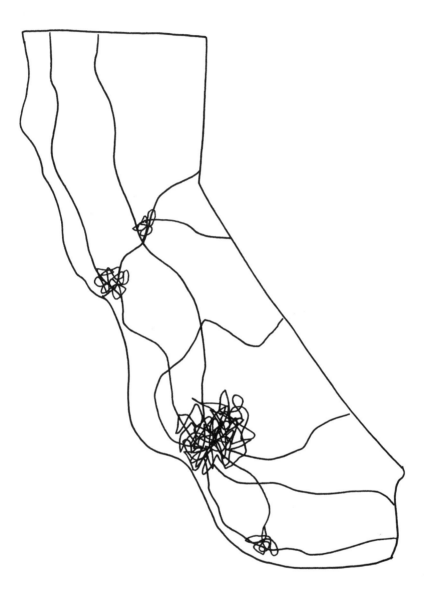

California Highways

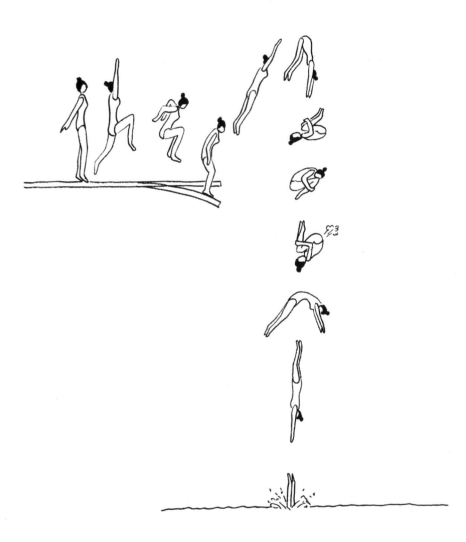

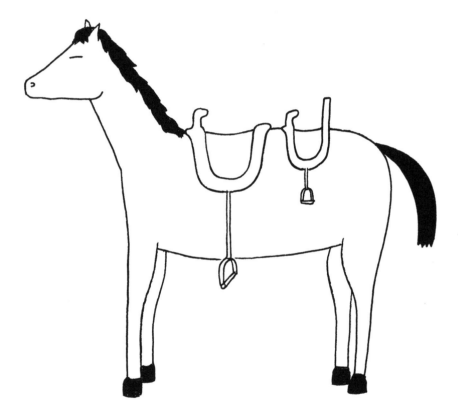

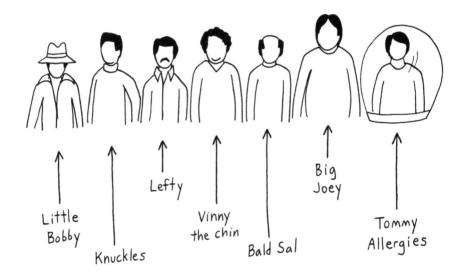

Little
Bobby

Knuckles

Lefty

Vinny
the chin

Bald Sal

Big
Joey

Tommy
Allergies

Sayings Missing One Letter

A bird in the hand is worth two in the bus.

If you can't eat them, join them.

A stitch in Tim saves nine.

Work hard, lay hard.

Ruth is stranger than fiction.

People who live in glass hoses shouldn't throw stones.

Follow your reams.

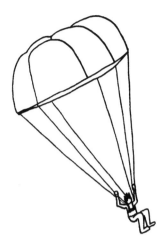

Turtle Flasher

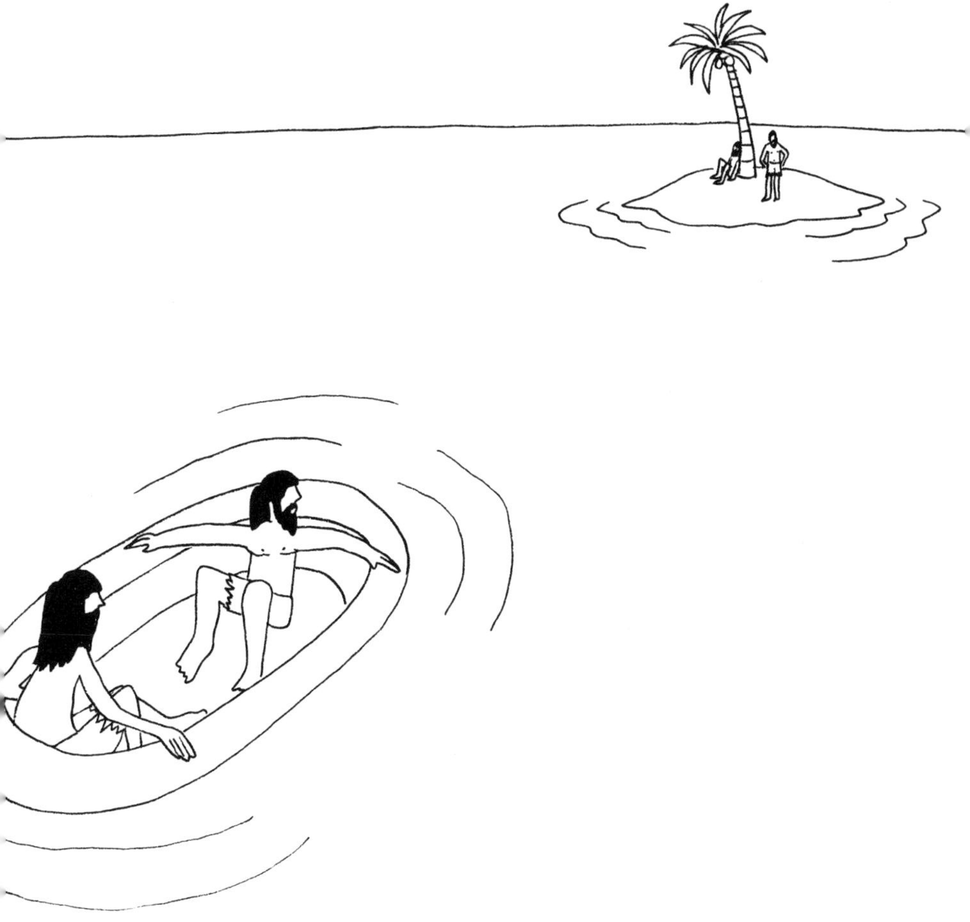

"Oh great. Another cliché."

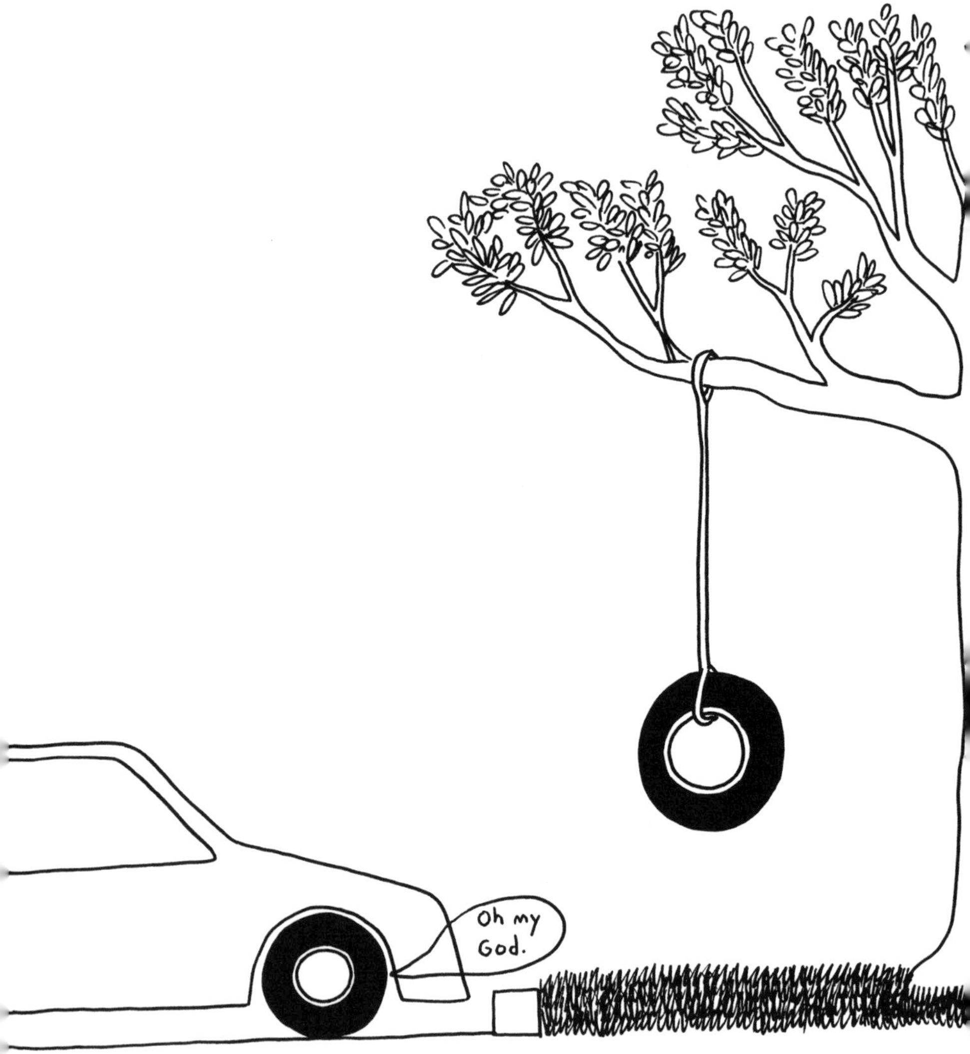
Oh my God.

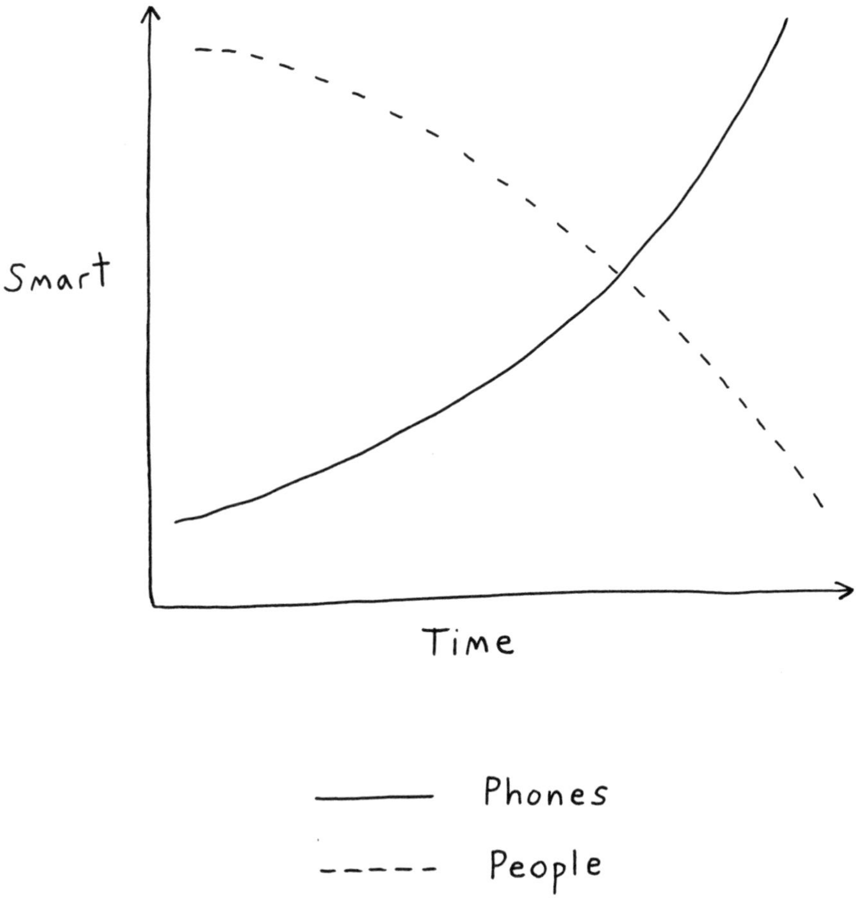
Smart
Time
Phones
People

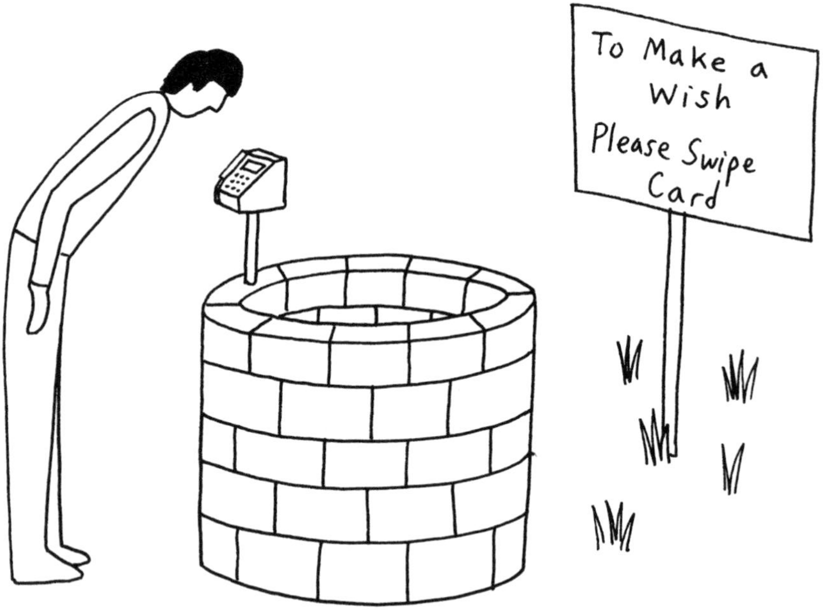
To Make a Wish
Please Swipe Card

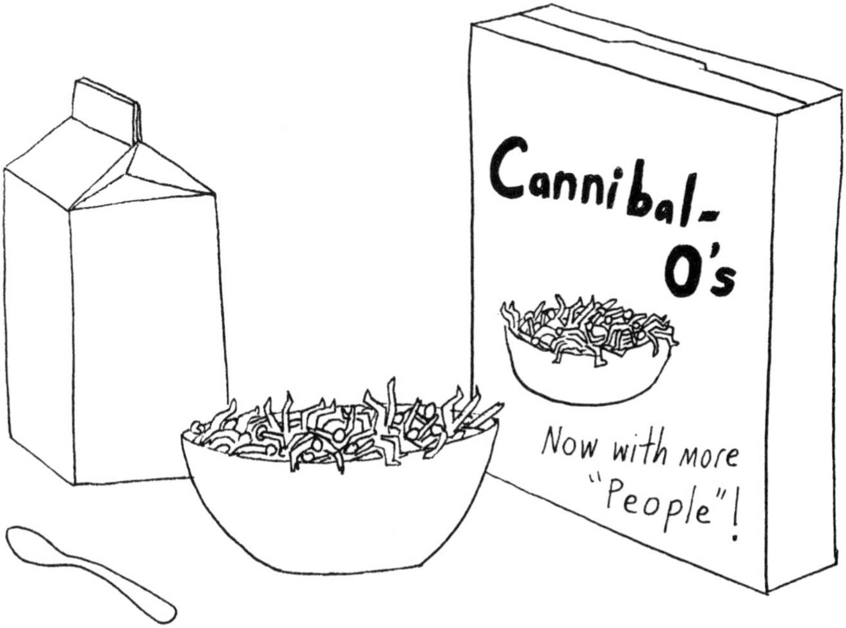
Cannibal-
O's
Now with more
"People"!

~~Writer~~ ~~Artist~~ ~~Designer~~ ~~Director~~
~~Philosopher~~ ~~Critic~~ ~~Blogger~~
Barrista

Vegetables
Sports
Ways
to
Die
Squash

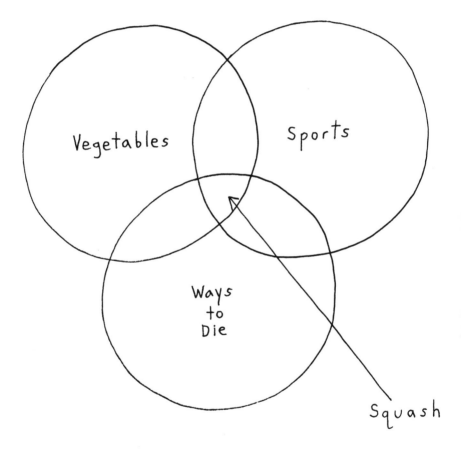

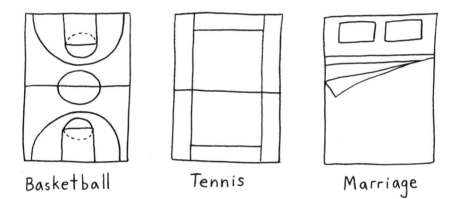

Basketball   Tennis   Marriage

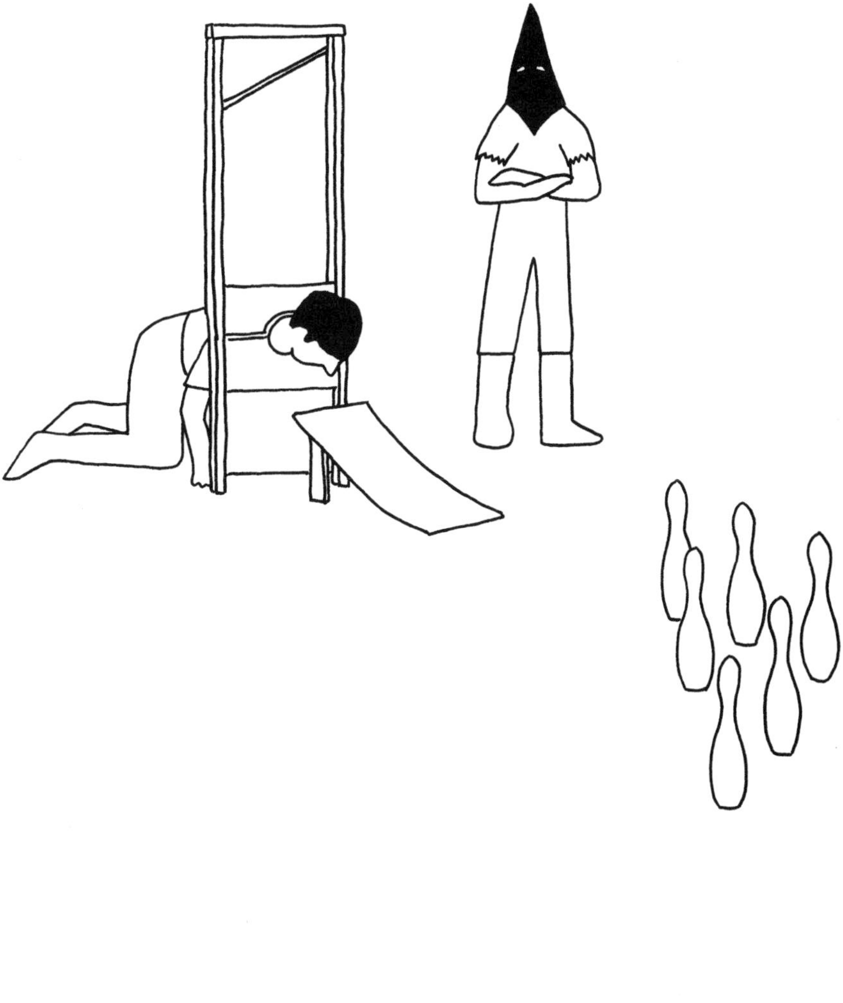

Rare Thoughts

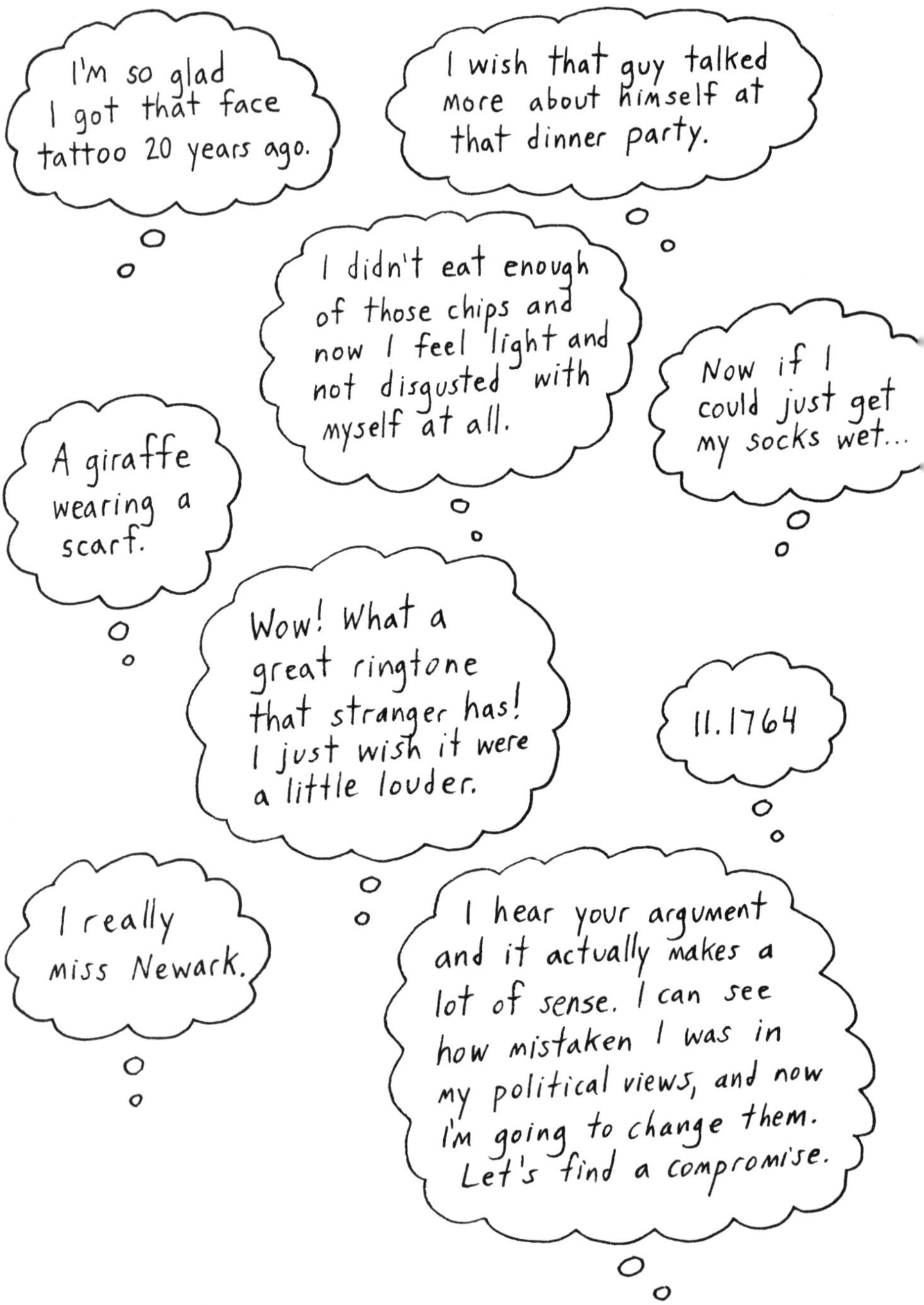
I'm so glad I got that face tattoo 20 years ago.
I wish that guy talked more about himself at that dinner party.
I didn't eat enough of those chips and now I feel light and not disgusted with myself at all.
Now if I could just get my socks wet...
A giraffe wearing a scarf.
Wow! What a great ringtone that stranger has! I just wish it were a little louder.
11.1764
I really miss Newark.
I hear your argument and it actually makes a lot of sense. I can see how mistaken I was in my political views, and now I'm going to change them. Let's find a compromise.

Unsuccessful Band

Bass   Drums   Keyboard   Bagpipes

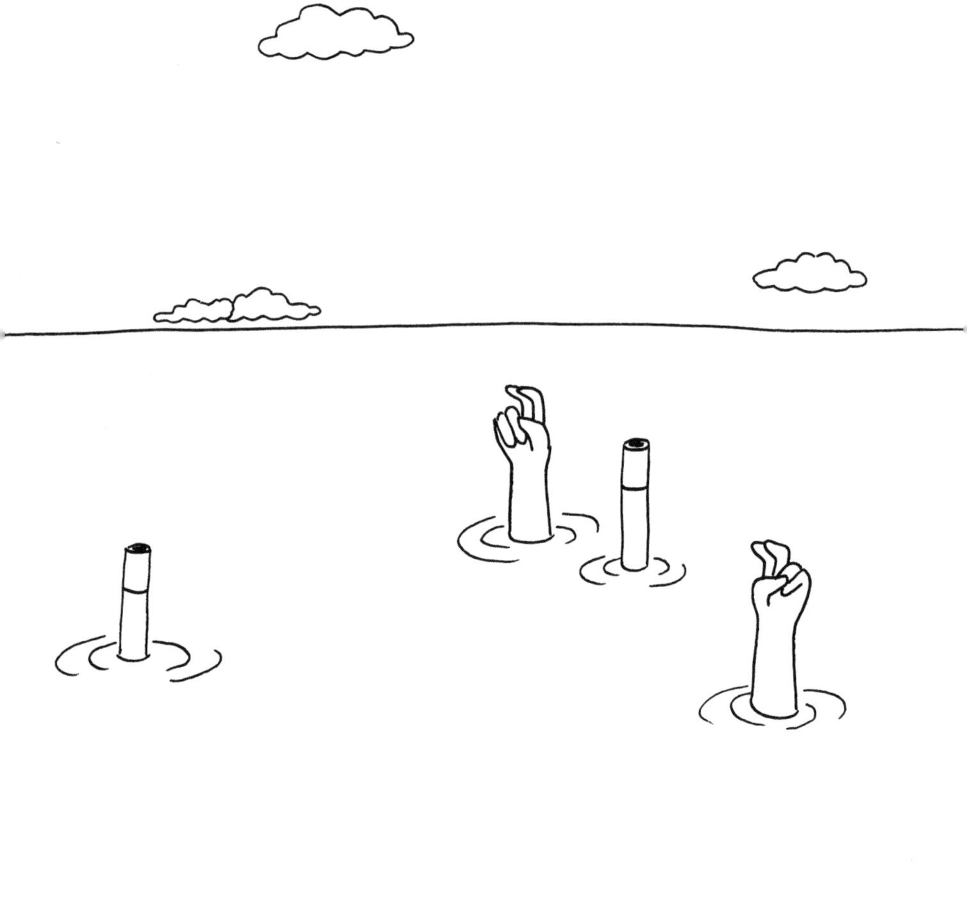

Snorkeler Uses Air Quotes

The Shits

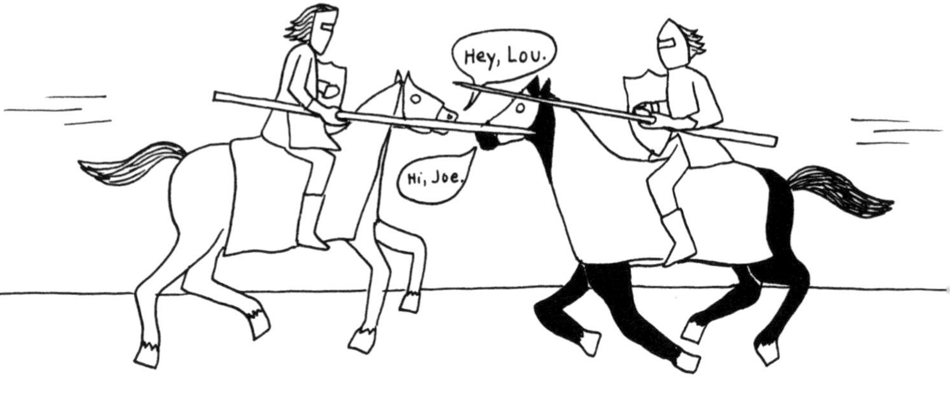
Hey, Lou.
Hi, Joe.

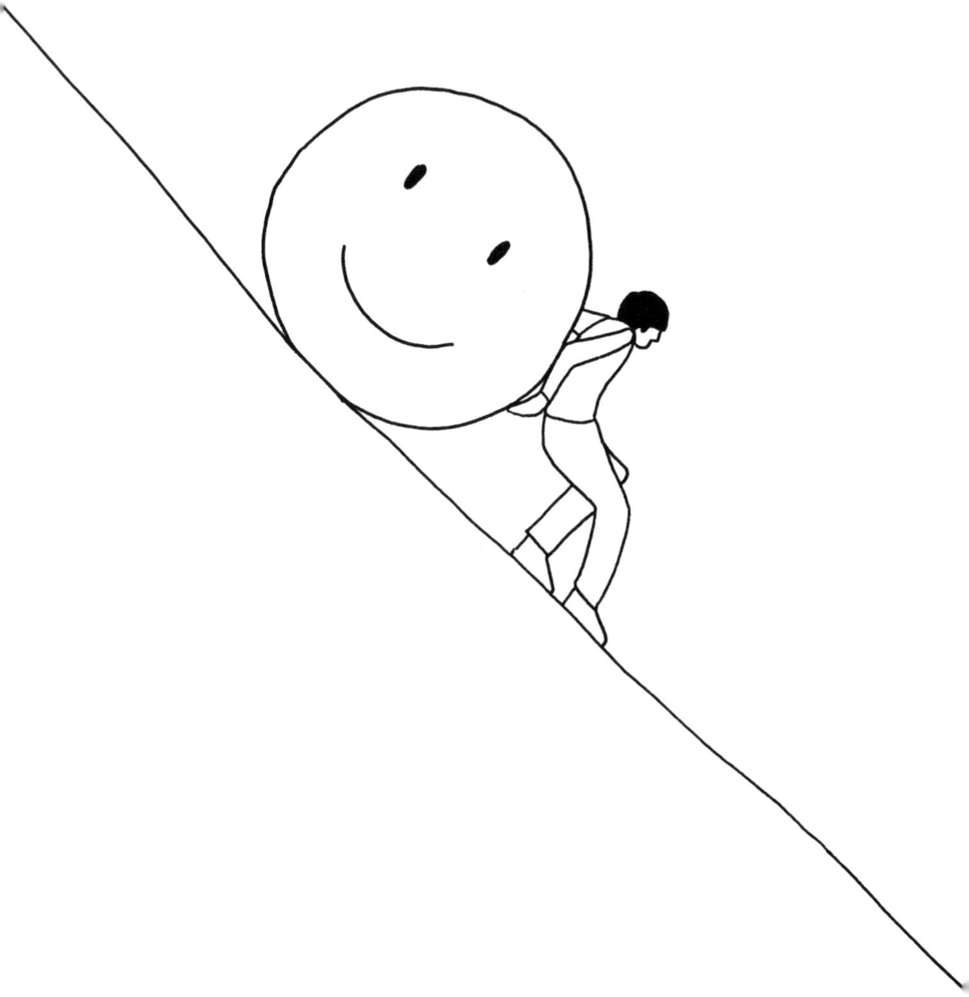

Which one of you is Chris?

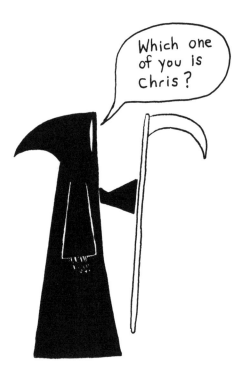

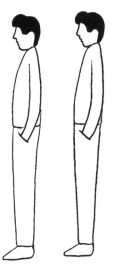

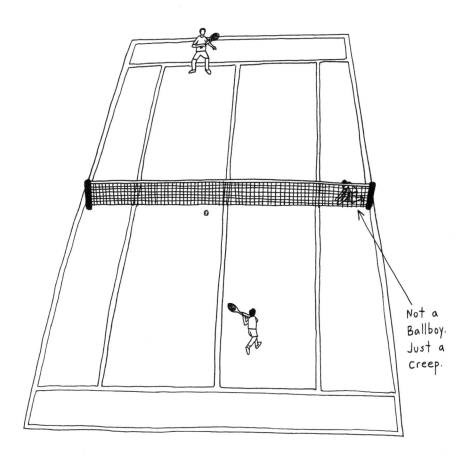

Not a
Ballboy.
Just a
creep.

Magician Masseuse

pretty pretty   =   kind of attractive

just just   =   barely fair

so so so   =   really very just okay

on on   =   not on "off"

drinks drinks   =   has alcohol

baby baby   =   pamper infant

poo poo poo poo   =   criticize feces

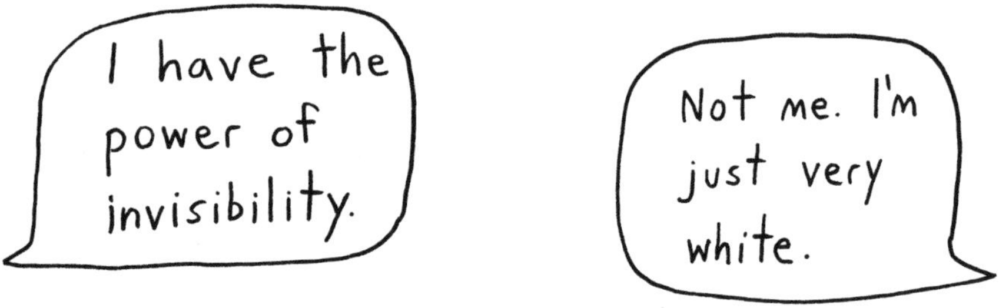
I have the power of invisibility.
Not me. I'm just very white.

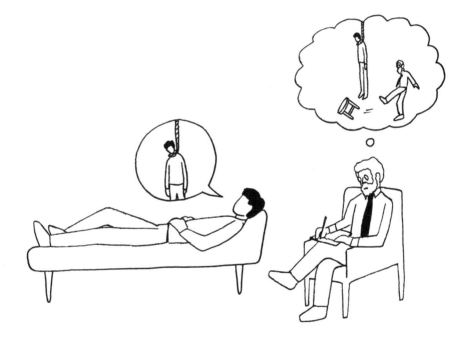

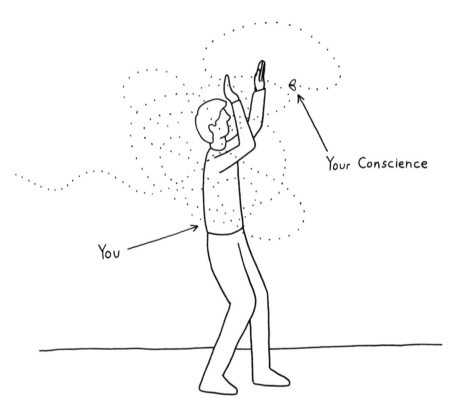

You

Your Conscience

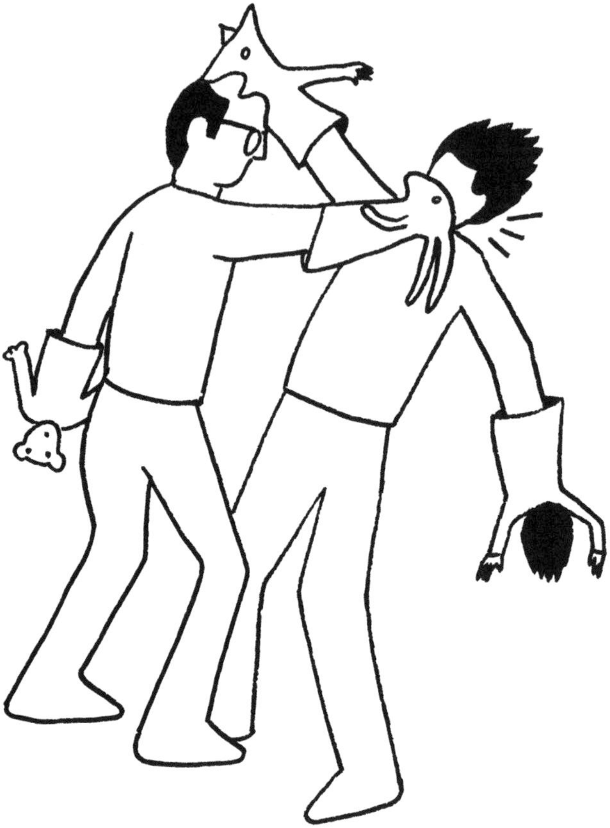

Puppeteer Fight

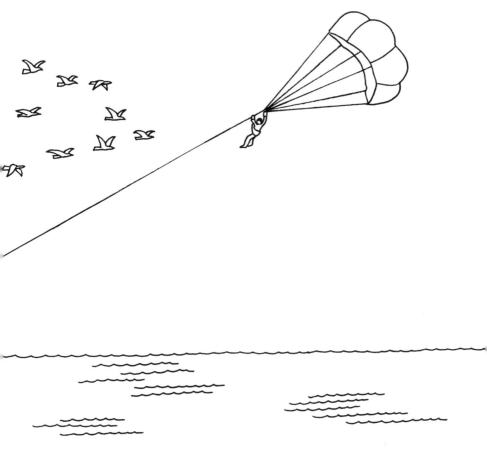

Things That Sound More Interesting Than They Are

Shoe Horn
Coaster
Parade Float
Layover
Hospital Gown

Cat Person
Titmouse
Illegal Alien
Everything Bagel
Air Hockey

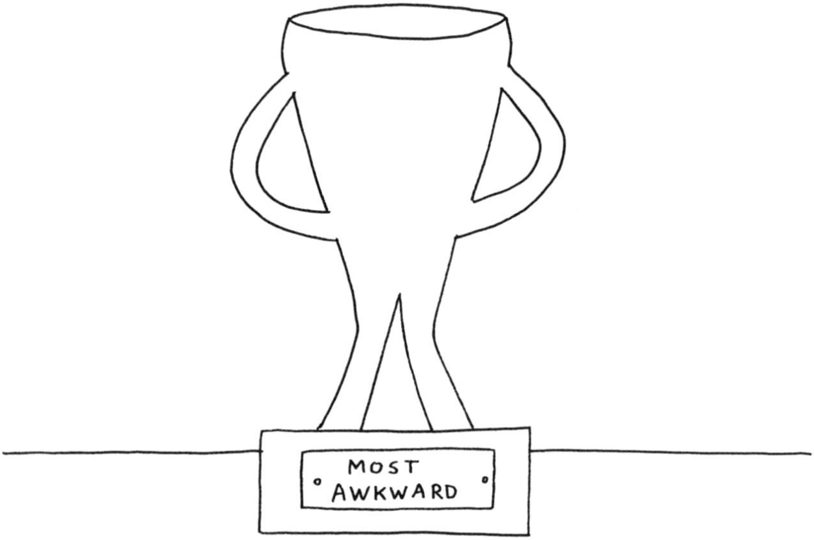
MOST
AWKWARD

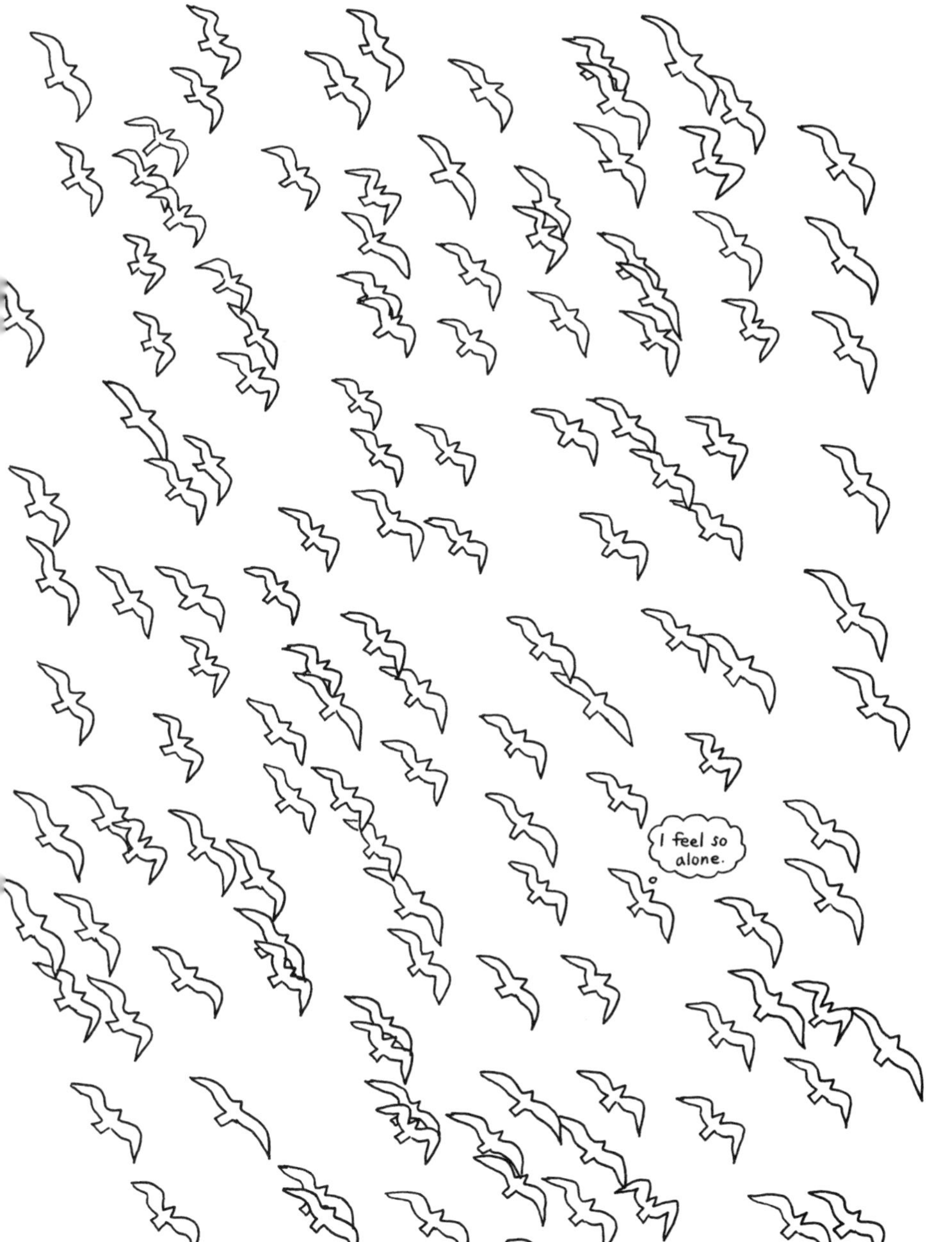
I feel so alone.

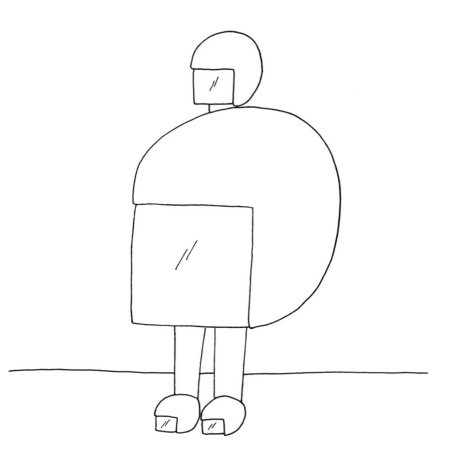

Helmet Man ™

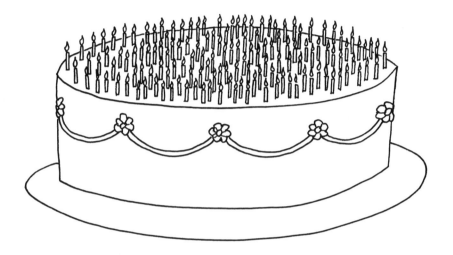

You have been alive too long

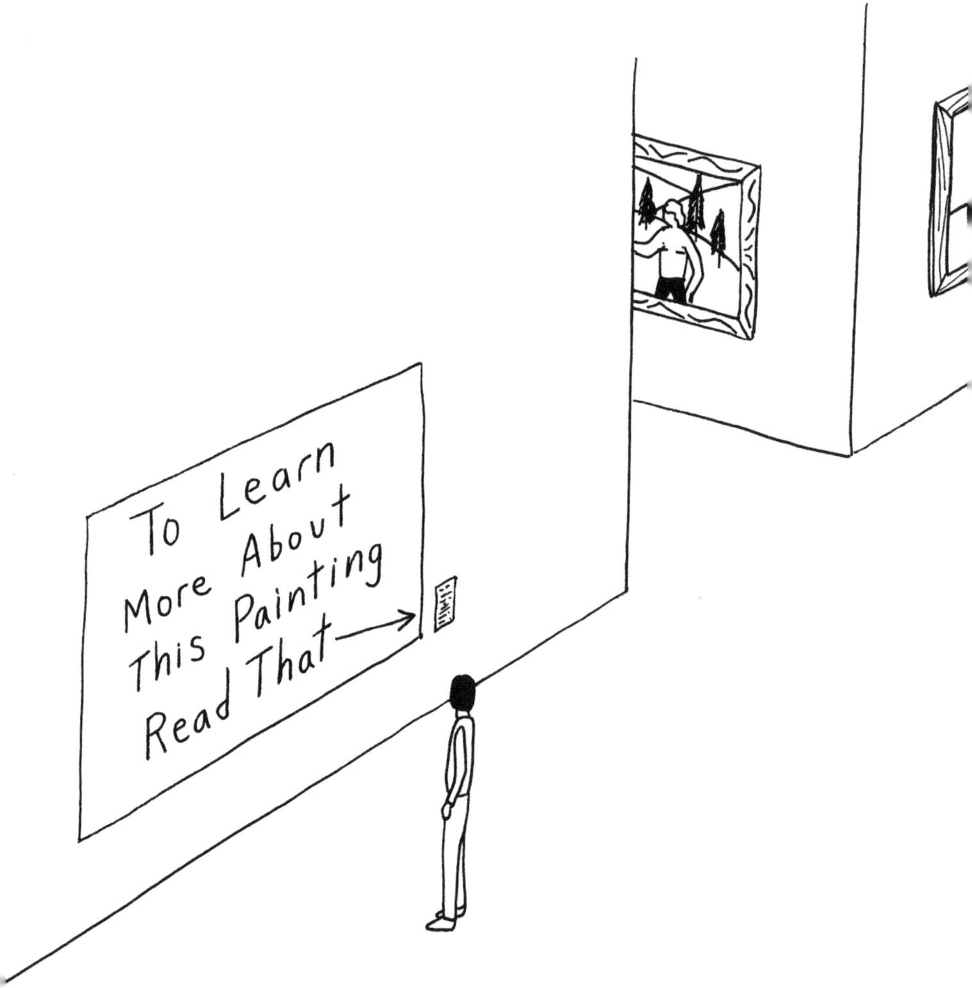
To Learn
More About
This Painting
Read That

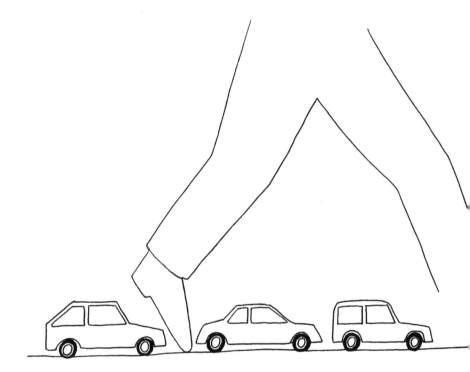

Giant is Polite

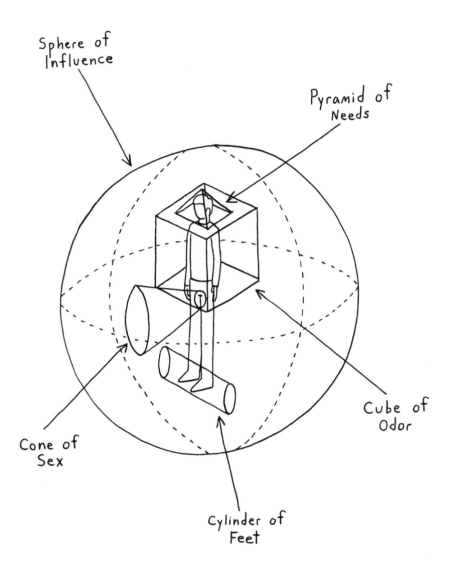

Sphere of Influence

Pyramid of Needs

Cube of Odor

Cone of Sex

Cylinder of Feet

Sorry for the mass e-mail...	=	No I'm not, and also I want something from you.
Don't take this the wrong way, but...	=	I'm about to insult you. There's no other way to take it.
Please don't hate me...	=	You should start hating me during this sentence.
Can I ask you a question?	=	Can I ask you another question after this one?
I'm not ready to be in a relationship right now	=	...with you, but I would totally with some I actually like.
Bro,...	=	I'm dumb,...
Quite frankly	=	I'm about to lie
I hate to break it to you	=	I'm totally okay with breaking it to you. In fact, I kind of like it.

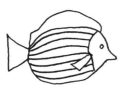

Your Fish Don't Know You

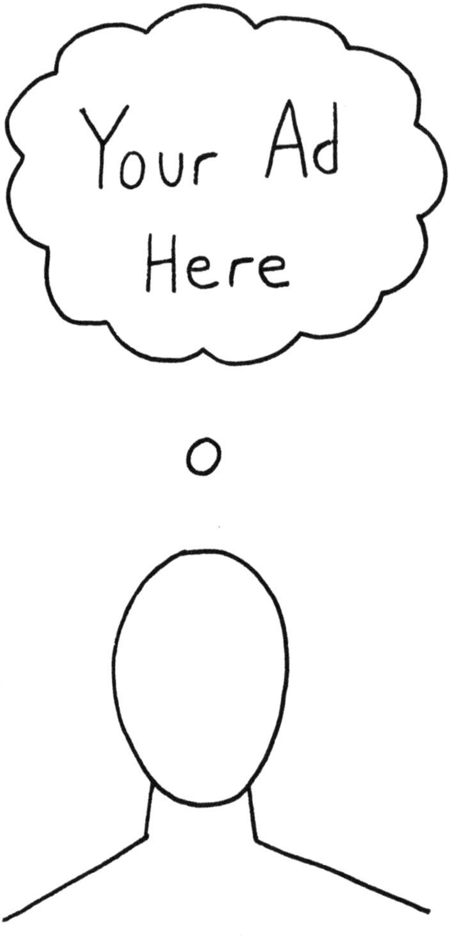
Your Ad
Here

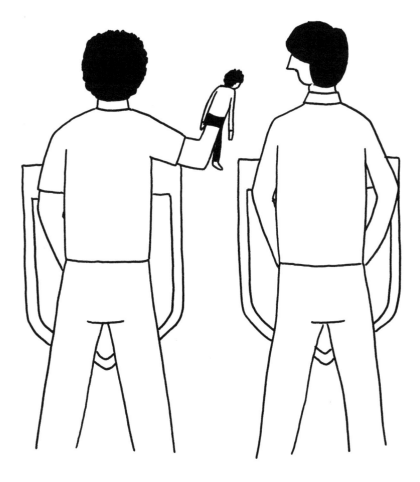

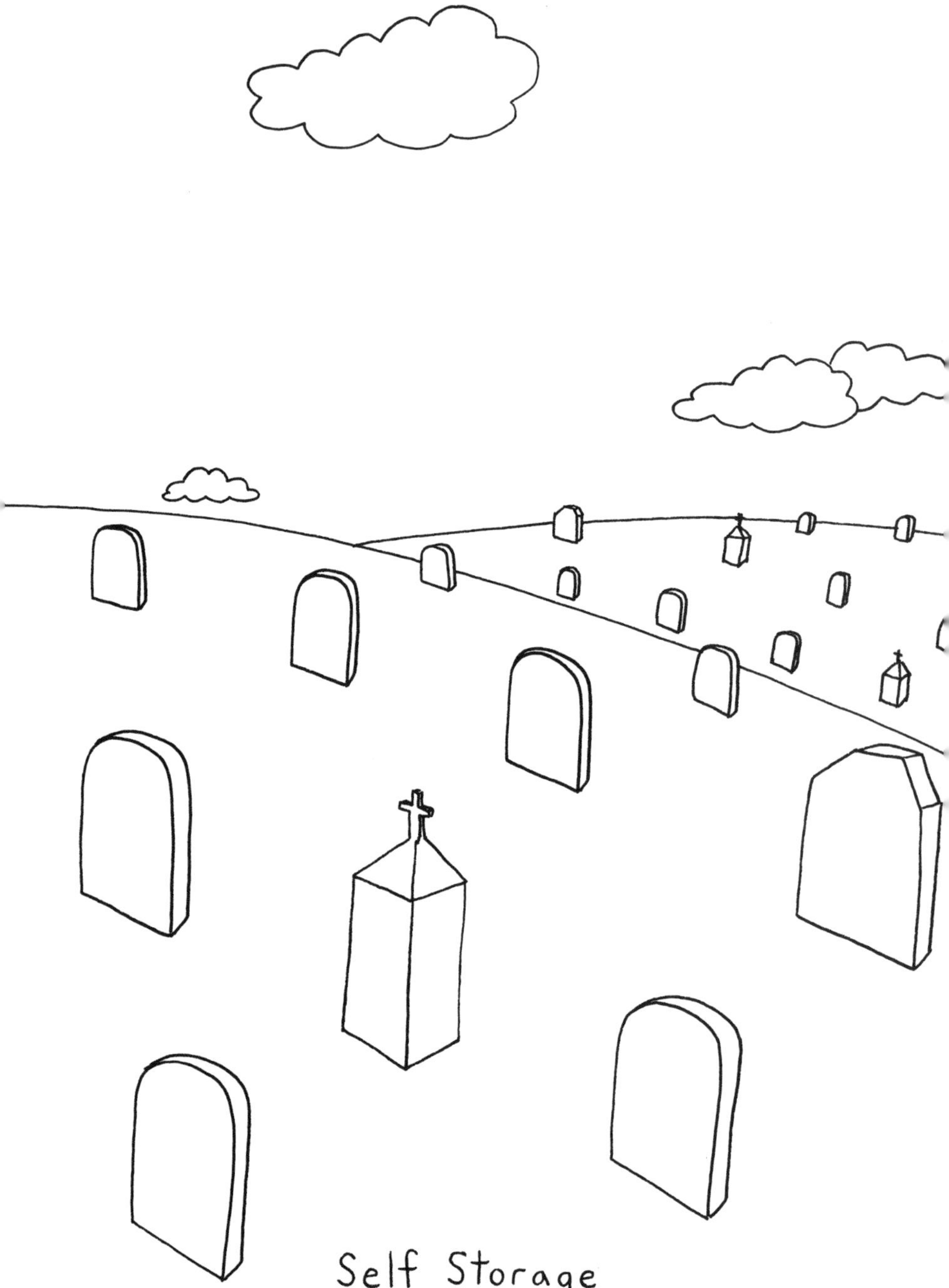

Self Storage

Shit.

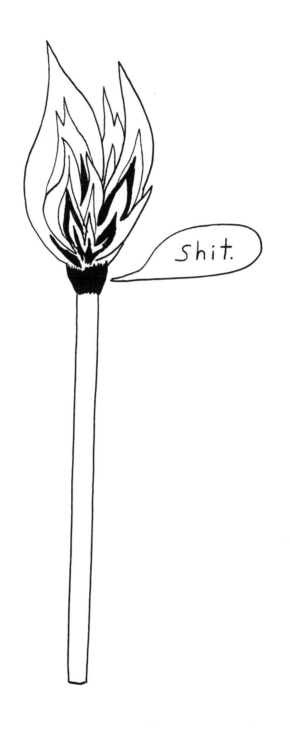

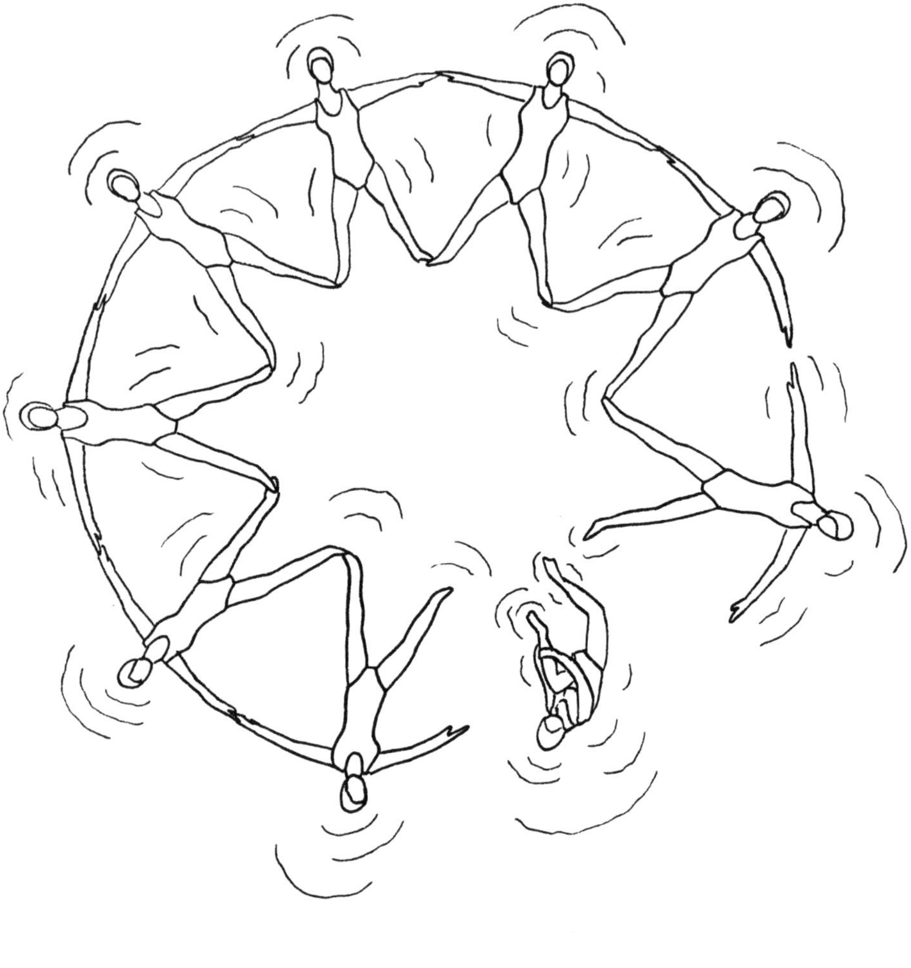

(cramp)

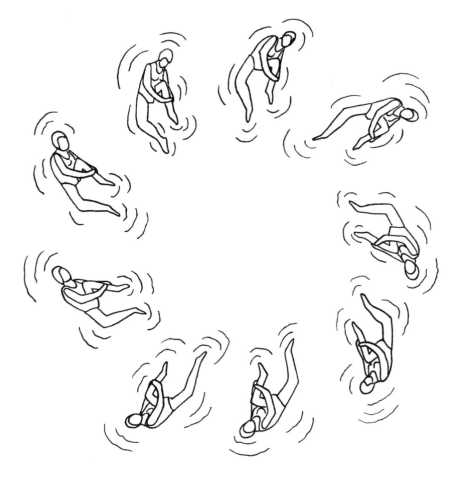

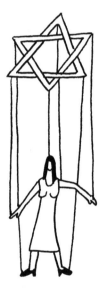
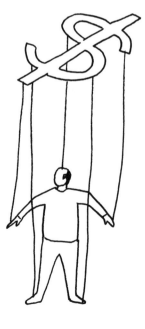

(Missing Contact Lens)

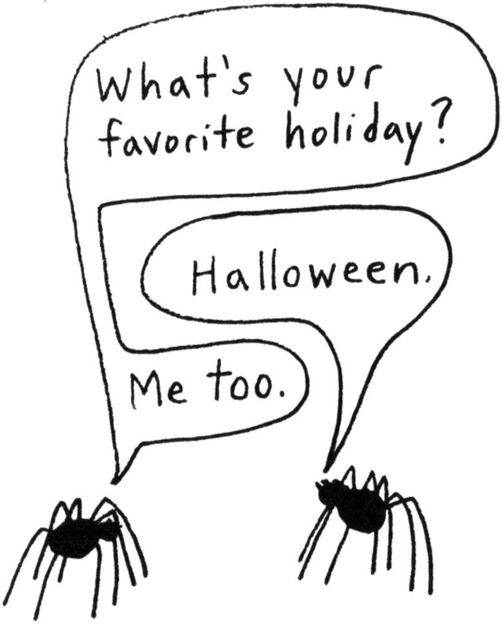
What's your favorite holiday?
Halloween.
Me too.

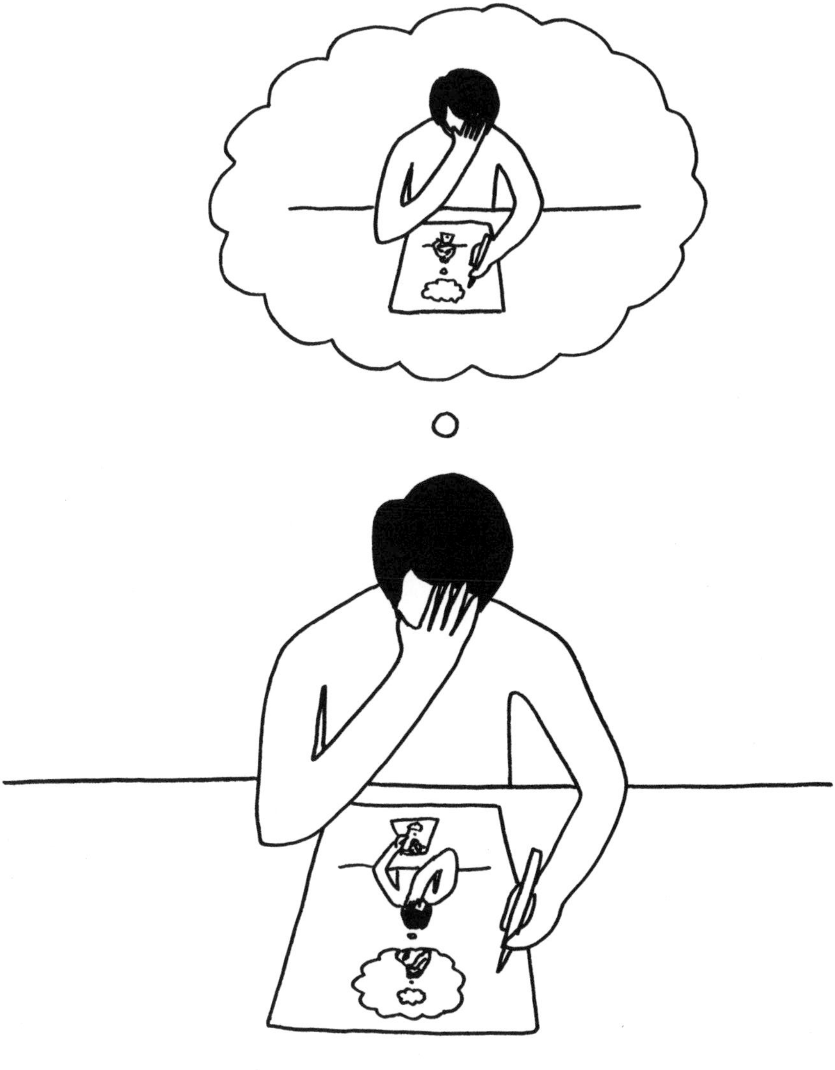

Character is late for drawing

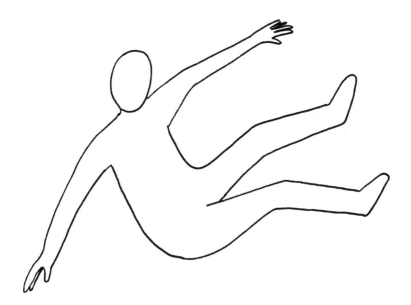

↑ Fun   ↓ Danger

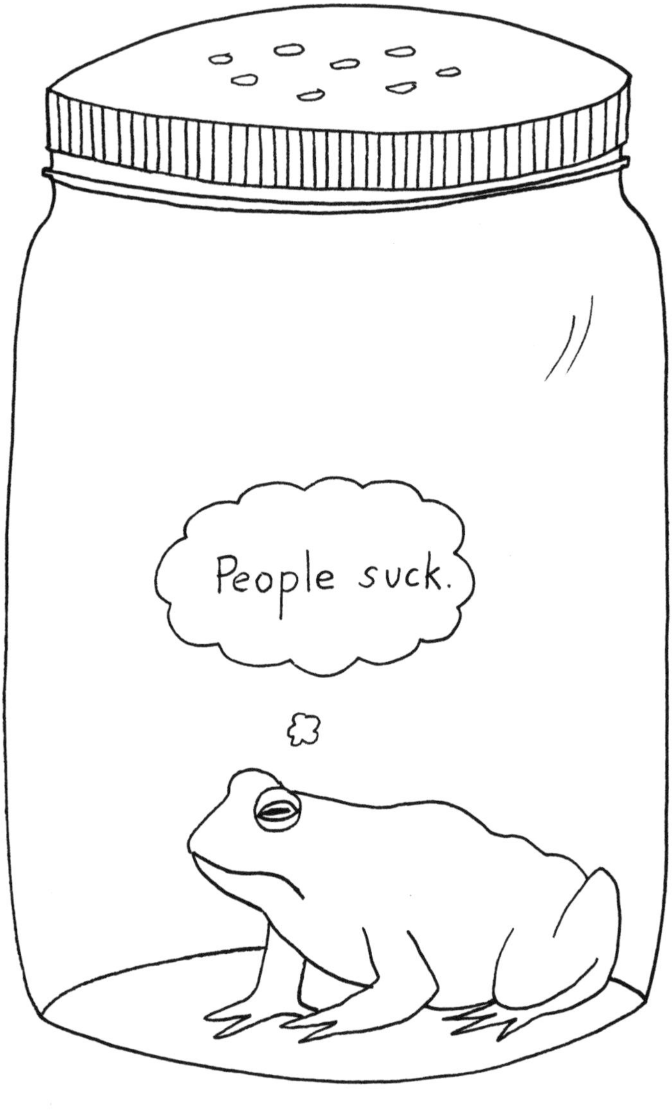
People suck.

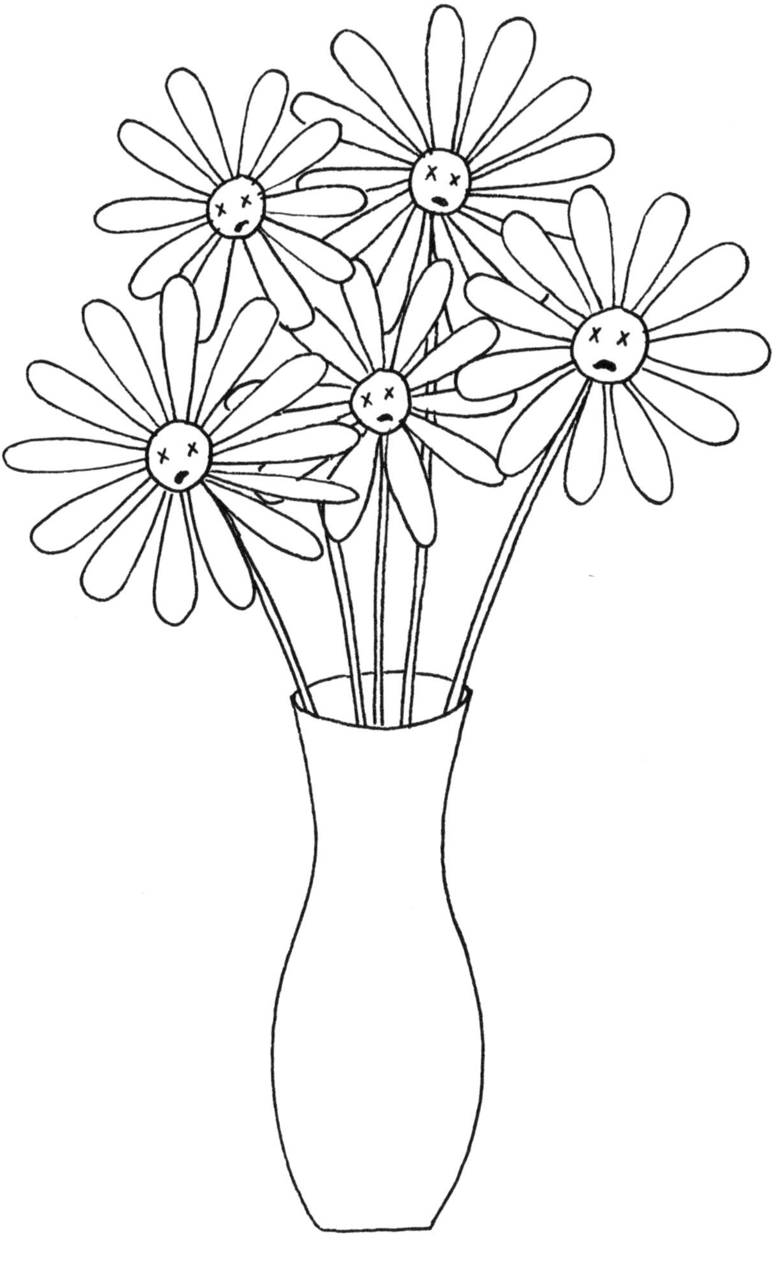

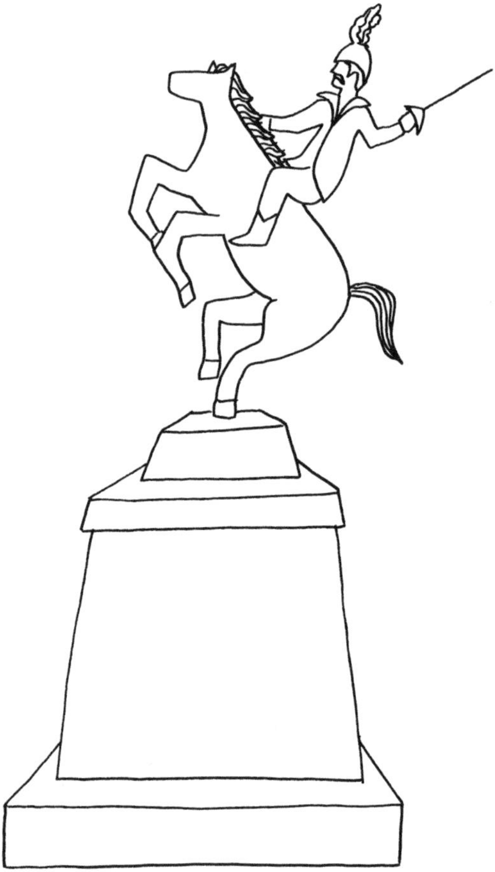

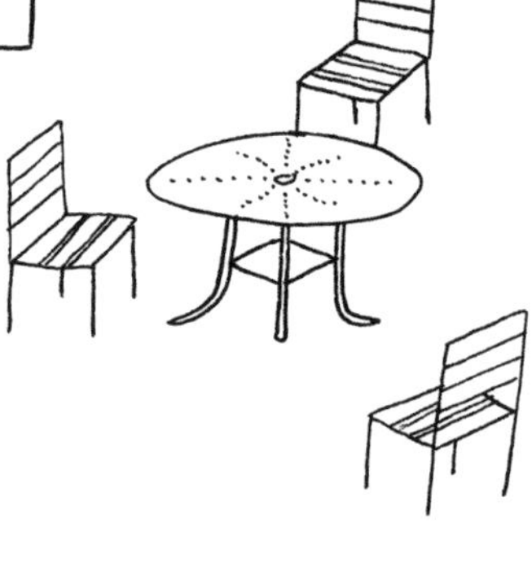

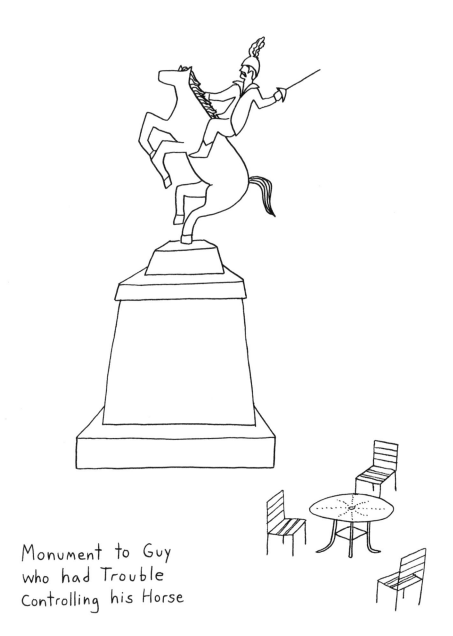

Monument to Guy
who had Trouble
Controlling his Horse

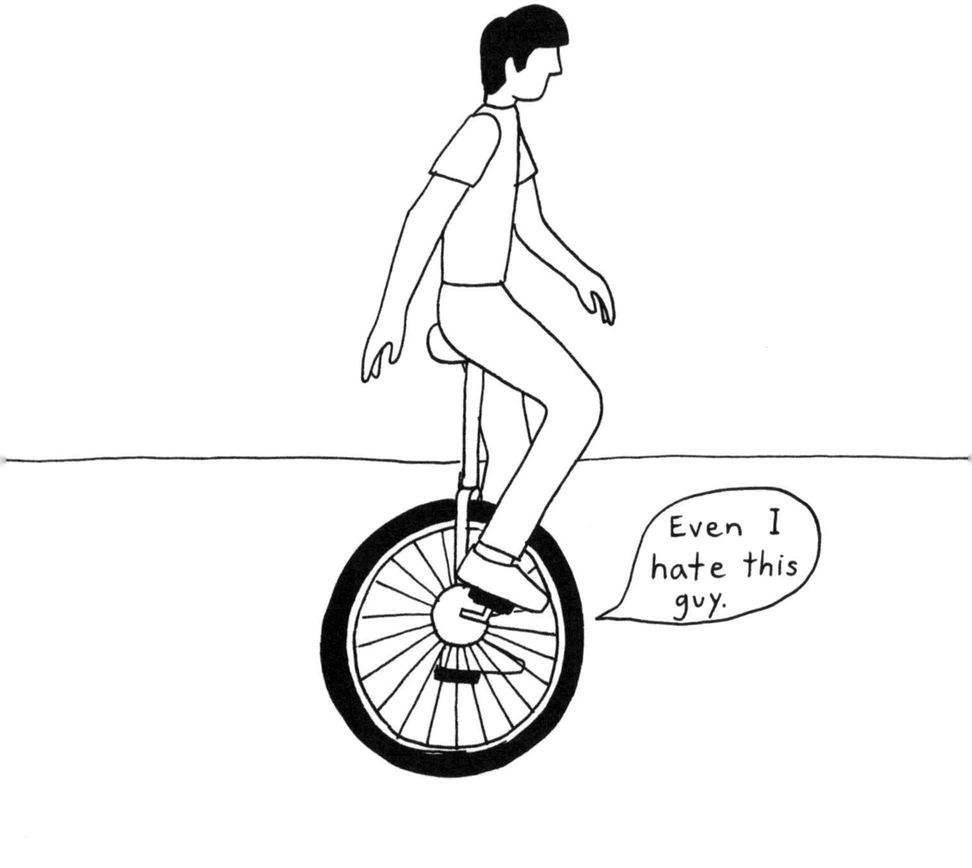
Even I hate this guy.

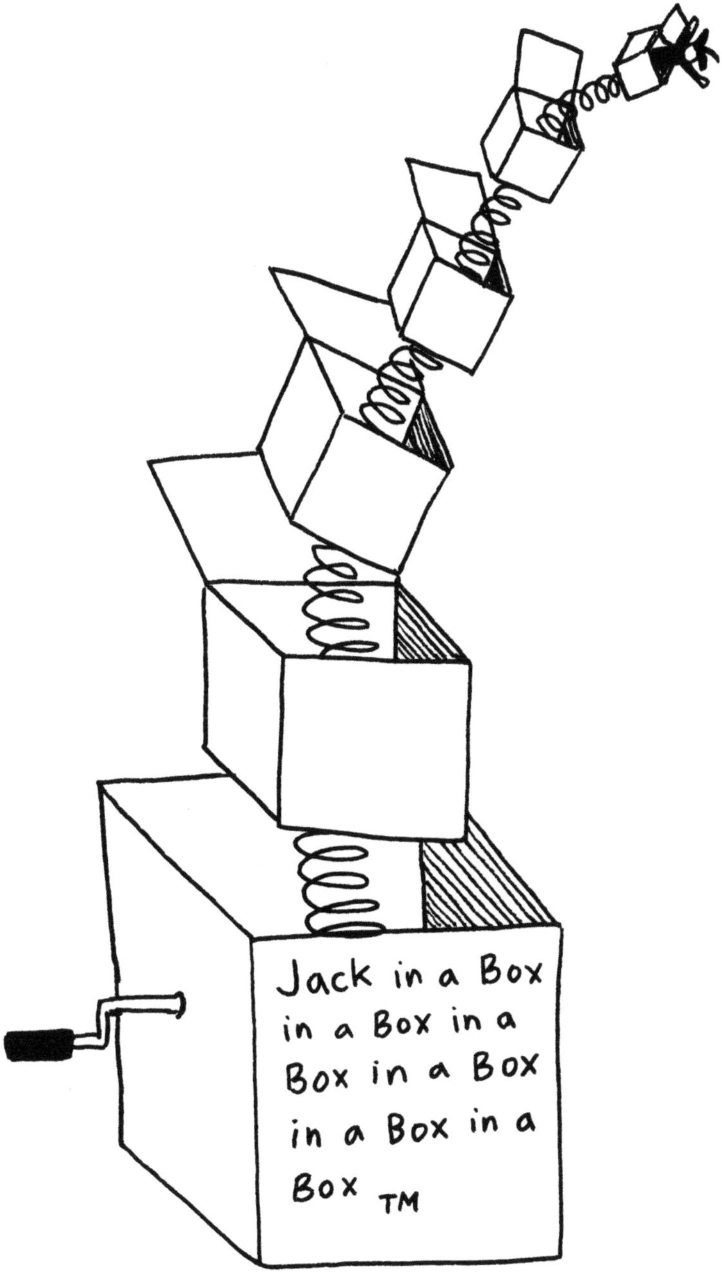
Jack in a Box
in a Box in a
Box in a Box
in a Box in a
Box TM

Products

1. Scented Pajamas
2. Edible Greeting Card
3. Inflatable Paperweight
4. Tandem Unicycle
5. Salad Spork
6. Whoopee Cushion Toilet Seat
7. Clear Wallpaper
8. Rollergloves
9. Sideways Rocking Chair
10. Cuckoo Microwave
11. Reodorant
12. (D)ice Cubes
13. Pogo Cot
14. Wearable Firepit
15. Stationary Bike that moves

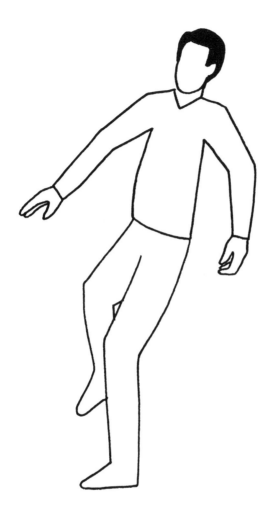

This Man is Not
Good at Dancing

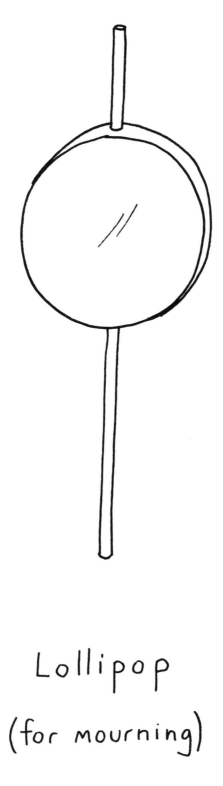

Lollipop

(for mourning)

Tiny Troll
Lives in your Drain

Gossip

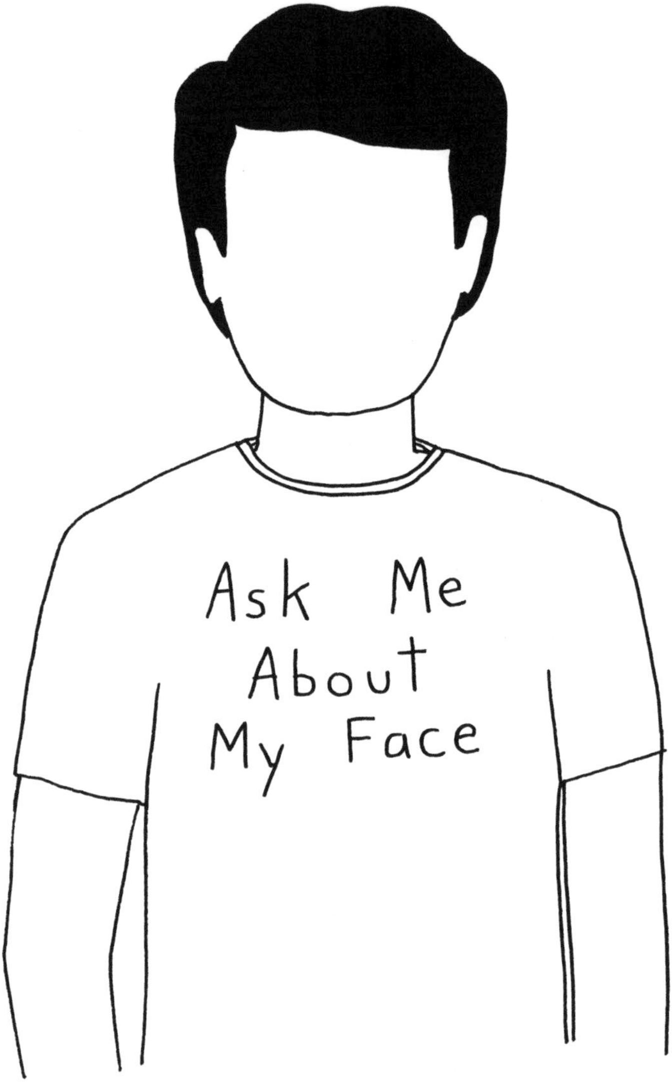
Ask Me
About
My Face

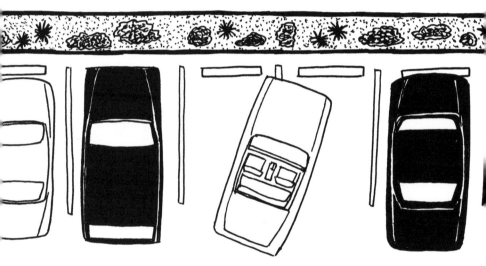

One reason why a person ends up in Hell

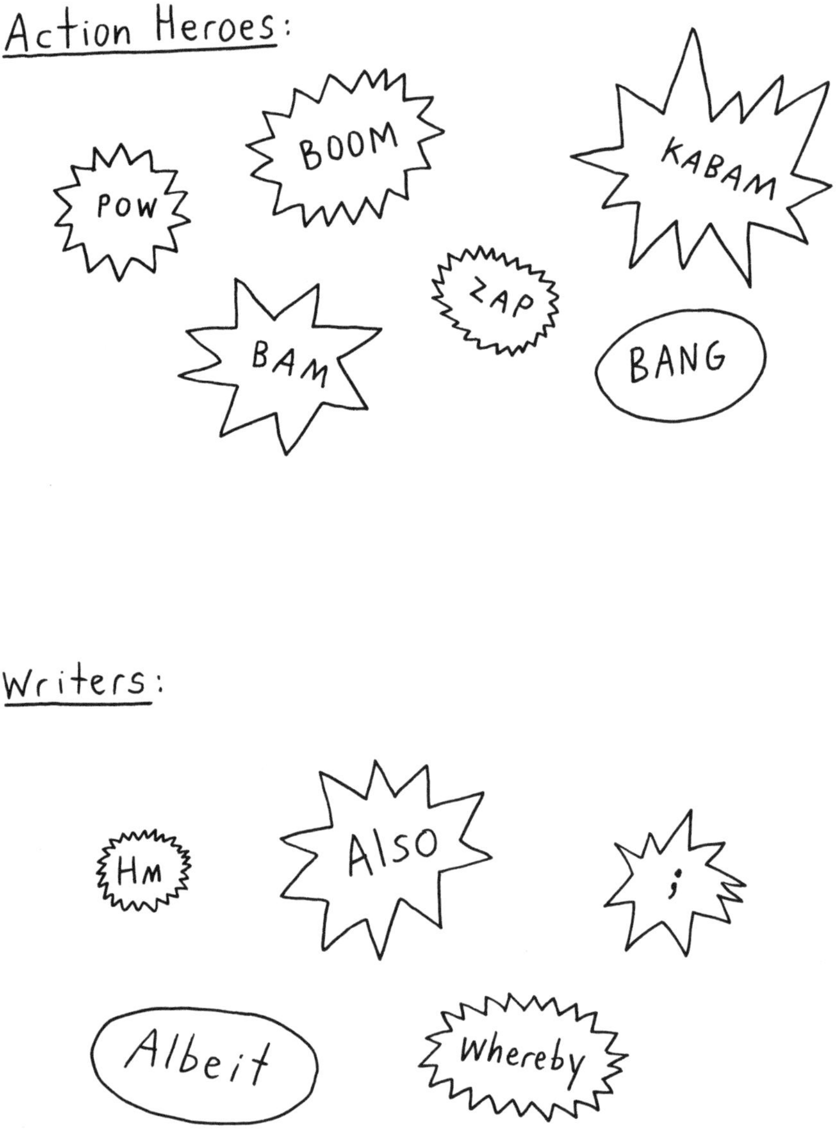
Action Heroes:
POW
BOOM
KABAM
BAM
ZAP
BANG
Writers:
Hm
Also
;
Albeit
Whereby

When wishes are not stated clearly enough

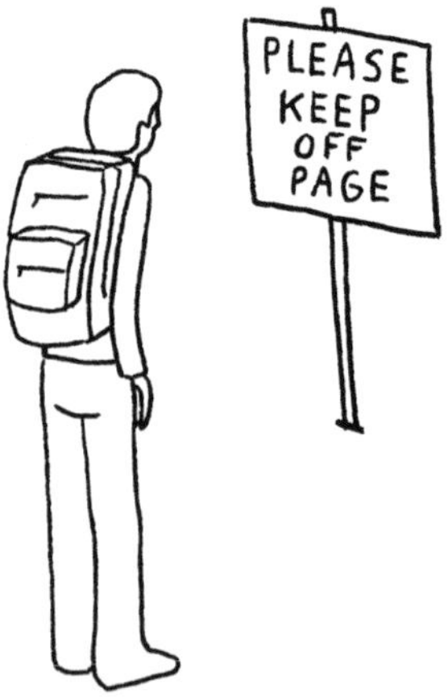
PLEASE
KEEP
OFF
PAGE

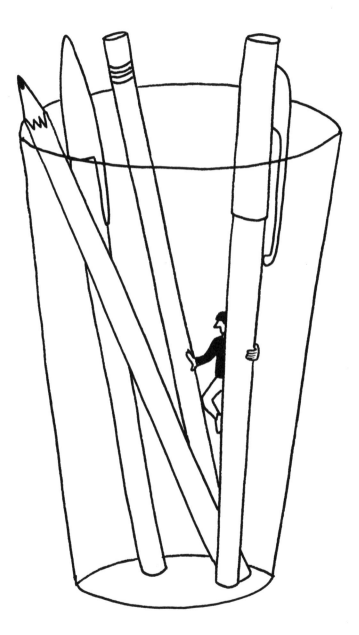

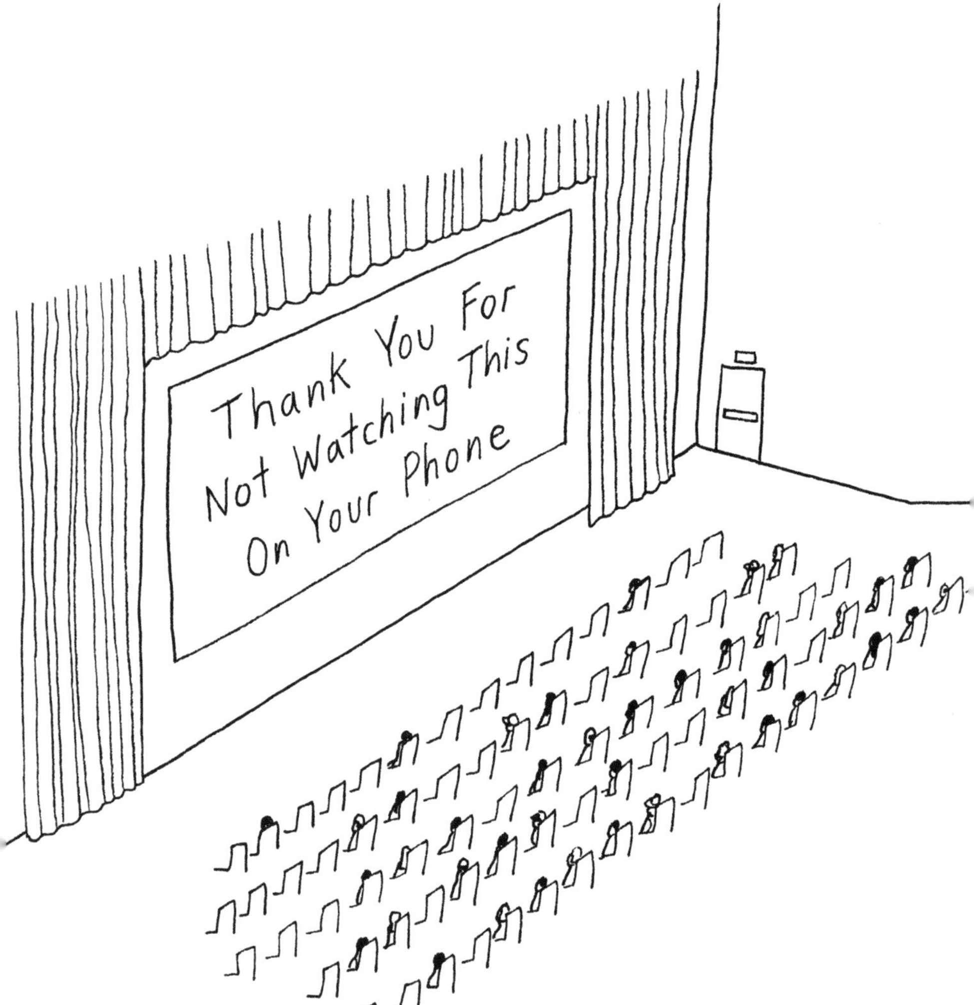
Thank You For
Not Watching This
On Your Phone

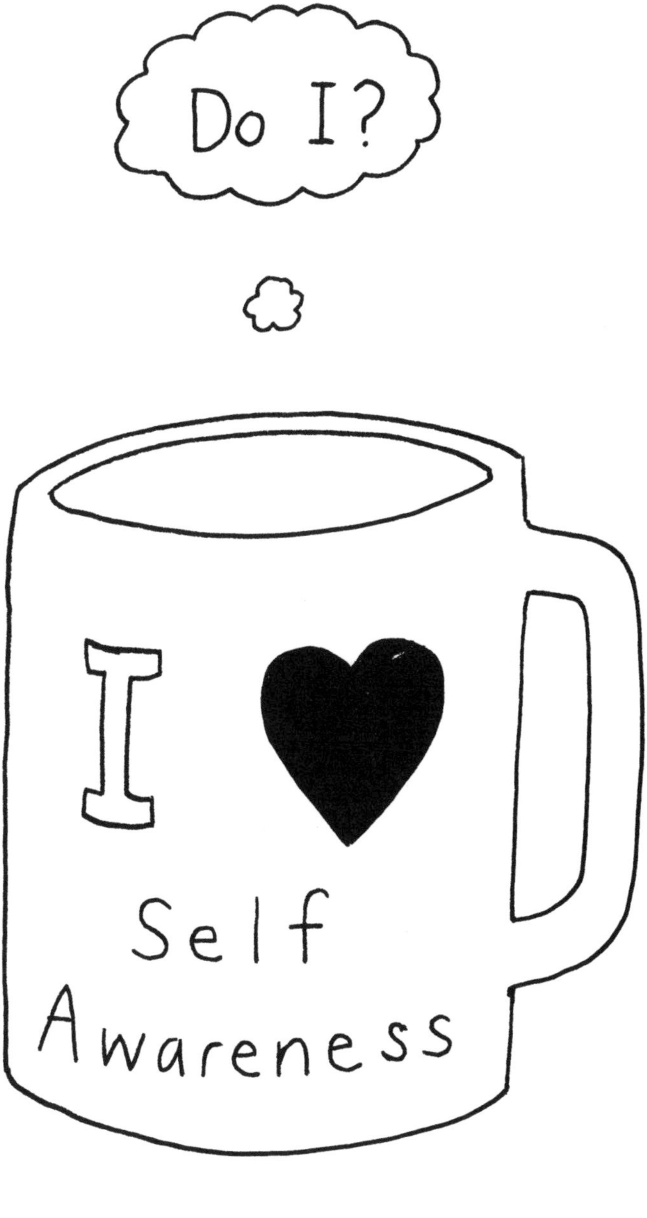
Do I?
I ♥ Self Awareness

"In your future I see--
... Huh... that's weird..."

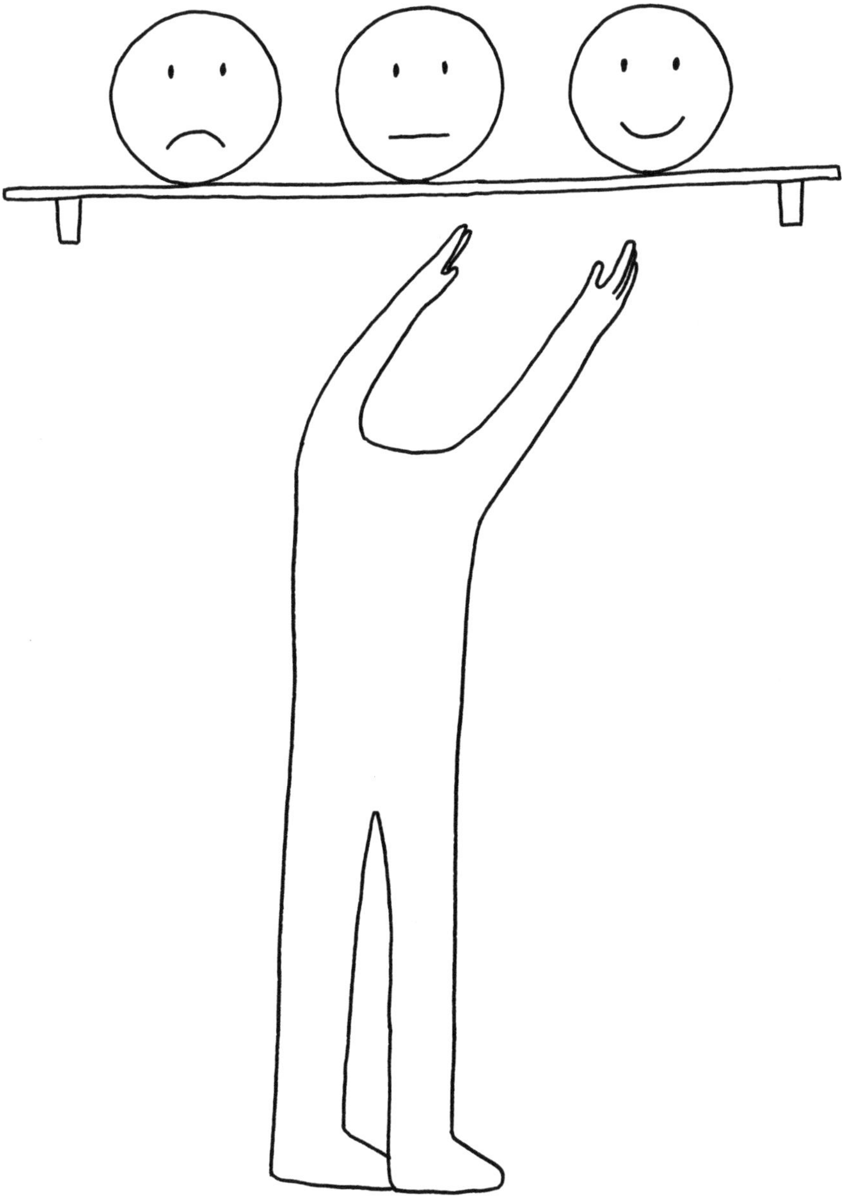

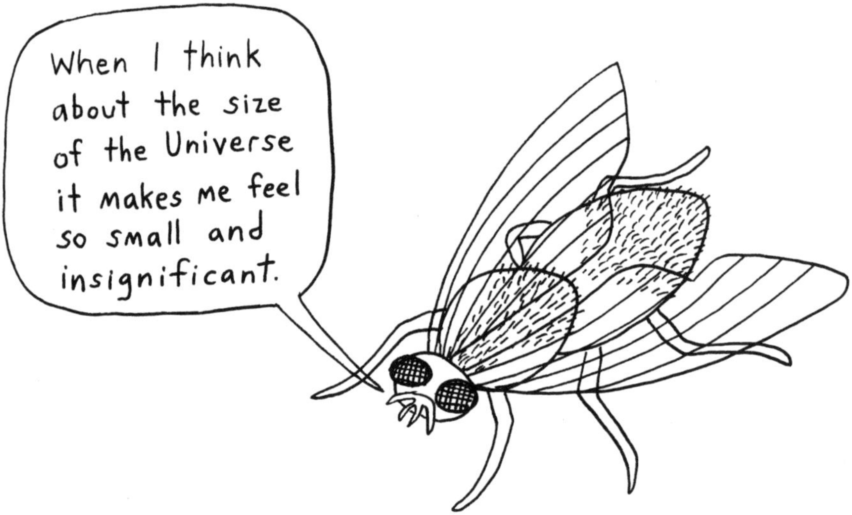
When I think about the size of the Universe it makes me feel so small and insignificant.

How Will You Be Remembered?

☐ "For my great selfies."

☐ "For my numerous posts and status updates on social media."

☐ "As a prolific tweeter."

☐ "My snarky blog."

☐ "For the exceptionally mean comments I posted about other people's work."

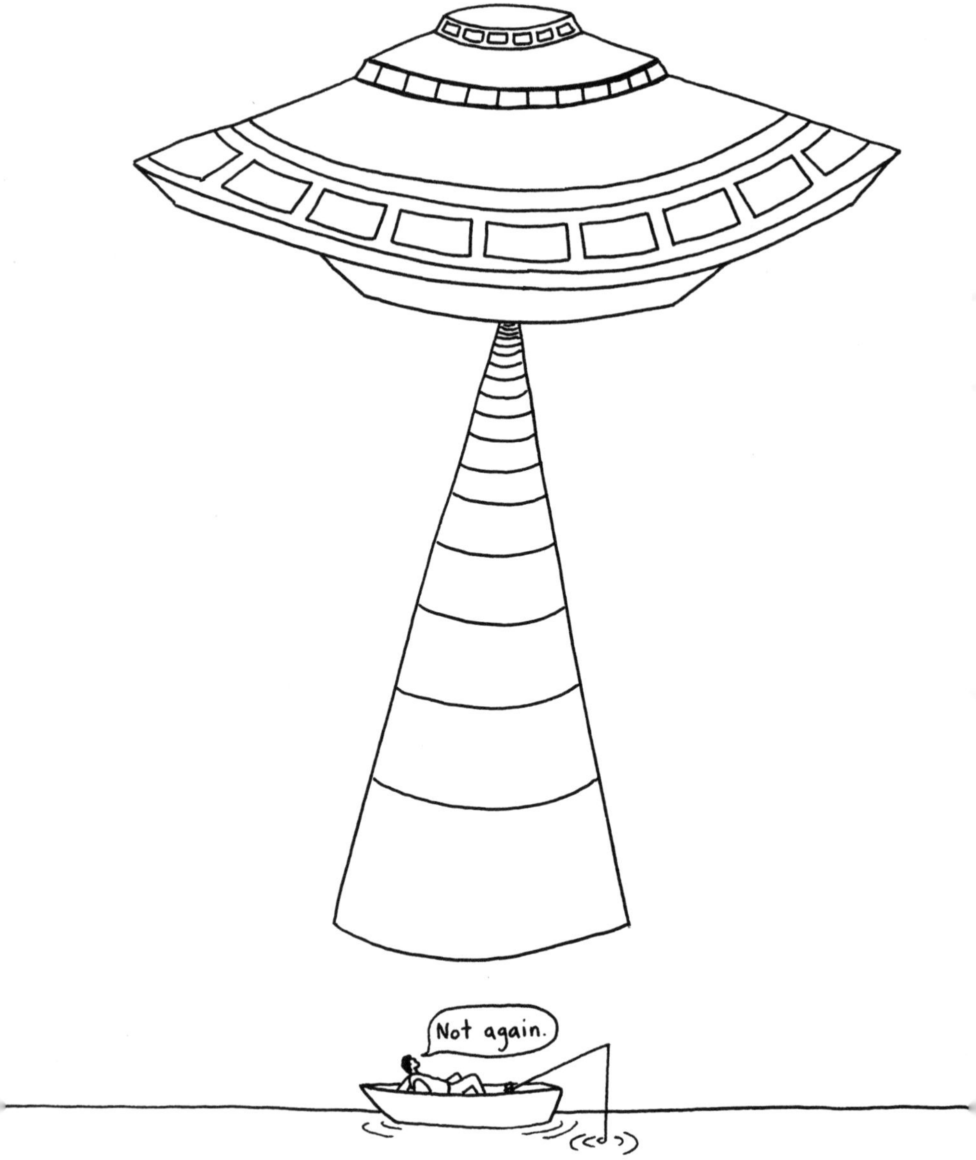
Not again.

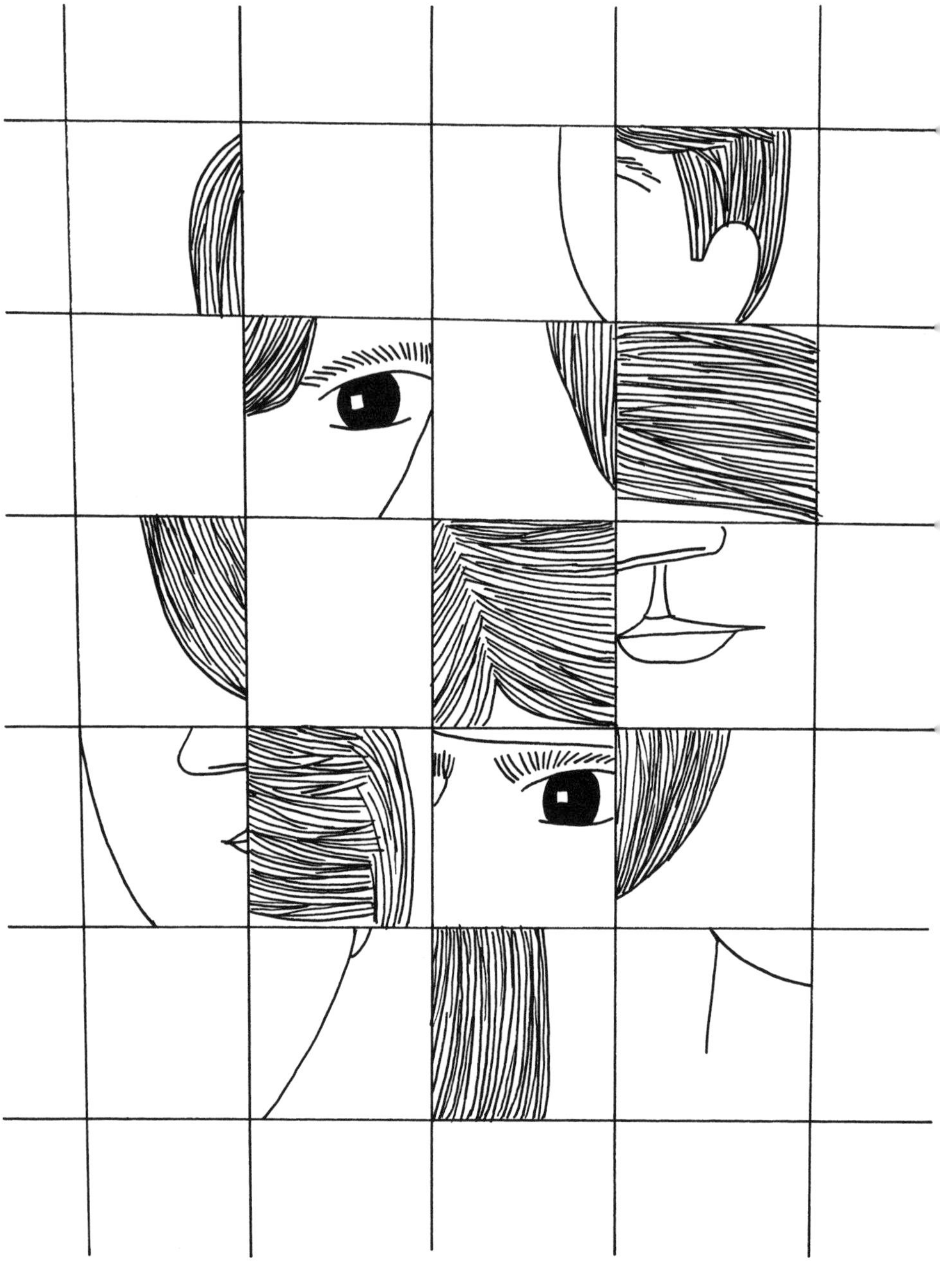

Slef-Pratorit

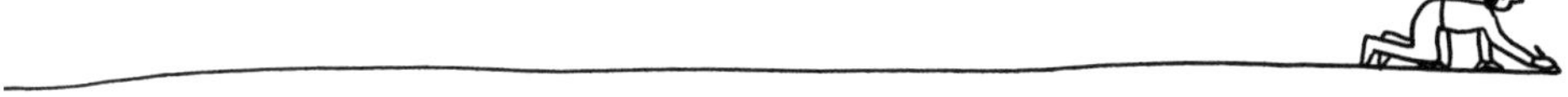